THE LOVE FOR THREE ORANGES

Vocal Score

SERGEI PROKOFIEV

Op. 33

DOVER PUBLICATIONS, INC.
Mineola, New York

Bibliographical Note

This Dover edition, first published in 2005, is an unabridged republication of *L'Amour des trois Oranges* originally published by Breitkopf and Härtel, Leipzig, 1922.

International Standard Book Number: 0-486-44169-5

Manufactured in the United States of America
Dover Publications, Inc., 31 East 2nd Street, Mineola, N.Y. 11501

Sergei Prokofiev

L'amour des trois Oranges

Libretto by Sergei Prokofiev and Vera Janacopoulos
Based on Vsevolod Meyerhold's adaptation of the play by Carlo Gozzi
Premiered: December 30, 1921 at the Chicago Opera House, conducted by the composer

Дѣйствующія лица.

Король Трефъ, король вымышленнаго государства, одежды котораго подобны игральнымъ картамъ	басъ
Принцъ, его сынъ	теноръ
Принцесса Клариче, племянница Короля	контральто
Леандръ, первый министръ, одѣтъ королемъ Пикъ	баритонъ
Труффальдино, человѣкъ, умѣющій смѣшить	теноръ
Панталонъ, приближенный Короля	баритонъ
Магъ Челій, покровительствуетъ Королю	басъ
Фата Моргана, вѣдьма, покровительствуетъ Леандру	сопрано
Линетта (принцессы въ апельсинахъ)	контральто
Николетта (принцессы въ апельсинахъ)	меццо-сопрано
Нинетта (принцессы въ апельсинахъ)	сопрано
Кухарка	хриплый басъ
Фарфарелло, дьяволъ	басъ
Смеральдина, арапка	меццо-сопрано
Церемонiймейстеръ	теноръ
Герольдъ	басъ
Трубачъ	басовый тромбонъ

Десять Чудаковъ	5 теноровъ 5 басовъ
Трагики	басы
Комики	тенора
Лирики	сопраны и тенора
Пустоголовые	альты и баритоны
Чертенята	басы
Медики	тенора и баритоны
Придворные	весь хоръ
Уроды Пьяницы Обжоры Стража Слуги Четыре солдата	нѣмые

Personnages.

Le Roi de Trèfles, roi d'un royaume imaginaire, dont le costume est celui des jeux de cartes	basse
Le Prince, son fils	ténor
La Princesse Clarisse, nièce du Roi	contralto
Léandre, premier ministre, habillé en roi de Piques	baryton
Trouffaldino, un homme qui fait rire	ténor
Pantalon, courtisan, intime du Roi	baryton
Le Magicien Tchélio, protège le Roi	basse
Fata Morgana, sorcière, protège Léandre	soprano
Linette (les princesses cachées dans les oranges)	contralto
Nicolette (les princesses cachées dans les oranges)	mezzo-soprano
Ninette (les princesses cachées dans les oranges)	soprano
La Cuisinière	basse enrouée
Farfarello, un diable	basse
Sméraldine, une noire	mezzo-soprano
Le Maître de Cérémonies	ténor
Le Héraut	basse
Le Trompette	trombone basse

Dix Ridicules	5 ténors 5 basses
Les Tragiques	basses
Les Comiques	ténors
Les Lyriques	sopranos et ténors
Les Têtes Vides	altos et barytons
Les diablotins (petits diables)	basses
Les médecins	ténors et barytons
Les courtisans	tout le chœur
Les monstres Les ivrognes Les gloutons Les gardes Les serviteurs Quatre soldats	muets

ЛЮБОВЬ КЪ ТРЕМЪ АПЕЛЬСИНАМЪ
L'amour des trois Oranges.

Прологъ.

Занавѣсъ опущенъ. Большой просценіумъ. По бокамъ просценіума двѣ башни съ перилами и балкончиками.

Prologue.

Le rideau est baissé. Grand proscenium. De chaque coté du proscenium une tour avec des petits balcons et balustrades.

Сергѣй Прокофьевъ
Serge Prokofieff
Op. 33.
1919

3
Комики, врываются на просценіумъ изъ лѣвой кулисы, размахивая хлыстами.
Les Comiques, se ruent sur le proscenium par la coulisse gauche brandissant des cravaches.
Ко - ме - - дій! Ко - ме - дій! Бод - ря - ща - го
Don - nez nous, don - nez nous de vraies co - mé -
Траг.
Trag.
мі - ро - выхъ про - блемъ!
et phi - lo - so - phiques!
Скор - би! У - бійствъ! Стра -
Meur - tres, dou - leurs, des
Ком.
Com.
смѣ - ха! О - здо - ров - ля - ю - ща - го смѣ - ха!
di - es! Du rire jo - yeux, du rire so - no - re!
да - ю - щихъ от - цовъ!
â - mes tor - tu - rées!
pizz, Ob., Cor.
4
До - воль - но тра - ге - дій!
As - sez de tra - gi - que!
Нападаютъ на Комиковъ.
Attaquant les Comiques.
До - воль - но смѣ - ха!
As - sez de ri - re!
Fiati e pizz.

5
Отступая передъ Трагиками къ лѣвой кулисѣ.
Reculant devant les Tragiques vers la coulisse gauche.
Ком.
Com.
Дай - те ра-дост - на-го!
De la gai - té sai-ne!
Размахивая зонтиками и тѣсня Комиковъ влѣво.
Agitant les parapluies et refoulant les Comiques à gauche.
Траг.
Trag.
Дай - - - - - - - те глу - бо - ка - го!
Non, des tra-gé - dies pro-fondes!
Зу - бо -
Mi - sé -
T-ni.
f
fp
p
Лирики, появляются изъ правой кулисы съ зелеными вѣтками.
Les Lyriques, sortant de la coulisse droite avec des branches vertes.
Лирики, ни на кого не нападая, занимаютъ середину просцеціума.
Les Lyriques n'attaquant personne, occupent le milieu du proscenium.
6
Драмъ, ли - ри - - - че - скихъ драмъ! Ро - ман -
Don - nez de vrais drames ly - riques, ro - man -
Отбиваясь у лѣвой кулисы.
Se défendant près de la coulisse gauche.
Ком.
Com.
Му - чи - те - ли! У - бій - цы!
Bour - reaux cru-els! Per - fi - des!
Траг.
Trag.
ска - - - лы! Бол - ту - ны! Тра -
ra - - - bles! Ta - pa - geurs! Du tra -
Fl.
etc.
Celli espress.

7
Лир.
Lyr.
ти - че - ской люб - ви!
tiques, é - mo - tion - nants,
Цвѣ - товъ!
des fleurs,
Лу -
la
Пустоголовые, съ тросточками, изъ правой кулисы, сразу нападаютъ на Лириковъ.
Têtes Vides, sortant de la coulisse droite avec de petites cannes, attaquent de suite les Lyriques.
Фар_совъ! Фар_совъ! За_нят_ной е_рун_ды!
Vi - te, vi - te, des far - ces a_mu_santes!
Ком.
Com.
До - лой! До - лой!
As - sez! A bas!
Траг.
Trag.
гич - на - го! Без - ыс - ход - на - го! Транс_цен_ден -
gi - - que! I_nex_tri_ca - - - - ble! Mé - ta - phy -
7
mf
f
m.d.

Лир.
Lyr.
ны!
lune!
Нѣж - ныхъ по - цѣ - лу - - - -
Des mo - ments d'ex - ta - - - -
Разогнавъ Лириковъ, сталкиваются съ Трагиками.
Ayant dispersé les Lyriques, attaquent les Tragiques.
Пусто-голов.
Têtes Vides.
Дву - смыс-ленныхъ ост - ротъ!
Des mots d'es-prit gri - vois!
На-ряд-ныхъ туа -
Donnez nous du
Ком.
Com.
До - лой! До - лой!
A bas! A bas!
Траг.
Trag.
таль - - - - - - - - на - го!
si - - - - - - - - - que!
ff
p

8
Лир.
Lyr.
евъ!
se!
Лю - - - - бов - - - - - на - - -
L'a - - - - mour rê - - -
Пустоголов.
Têtes Vides.
ле - - - - товъ!
lu - - - - xe!
Трагикамъ.
Aux Tragiques.
Вонъ меланхоликовъ!
Au diable, vieux croque-morts!
Ком.
Com.
Дайте намъ здоро - - ваго смѣ - ха!
Il faut de la joie et du ri - re,
Дайте намъ
de la verve
Накидываются на Пустоголовыхъ.
Se jettant sur les Têtes Vides.
Траг.
Trag.
Пошляки! Пошляки!
Fainéants! Débaucheurs!
Раз - - -
Têtes
8

Лир.
Lyr.
го то - мле - - - - - - ні - я!
veur et ten - - - - - - - - dre!
Пусто-
голов.
Têtes
Vides.
Вонъ глу - пыхъ ум - ни - ковъ! Хо - тимъ не
A la por - te, vieux cré - tins! Ne pas pen -
Ком.
Com.
ост - рыхъ словъ и ост - рыхъ по - ло - же - ній! Ко - ме - - - -
de l'es - prit et des su - jets com - ple - xes! Don - nez
Траг.
Trag.
врат - ни - ки! Без - дѣль - ни - ки!
vi - - - - des, sor - tez d'i - ci!

9
strin
Лир.
Lyr.
Мяг - - кой, меч - та - - - - - тель - ной
Des rê - - - - ves, des son - - - - - ges ly -
Пусто-
голов.
Têtes
Vides.
ду-мать и смѣ - ять-ся, и смѣ - ять-ся, и смѣ - ять - - - - - ся!
ser, ne pas pen - ser, mais ri - re, ri - re, ri - re, ri - - - - - re!
Ком.
Com.
дій! Ко - ме - - - - - - - дій! Дай-те, дай-те,
nous, don - nez nous du co - mi - que,
Траг.
Trag.
Па-ра-зи - ты! Па-ра-зи - ты! Па-ра-зи - ты! Тра - ге - дій,
Pa-ra-si - tes! Pa-ra-si - tes! Pa-ra-si - tes! Don - nez nous
9
strin
p cresc.
mf cresc.

gen - - - - - - - - - - - - do
Лир.
Lyr.
ли - - - - - - - - - ри - - - ки!
ri - - - - - - - - - - - - - ques!
f
Пусто-
голов.
Têtes
Vides.
Фар - - - - - совъ! Фар - - - - - совъ!
Don - - nez des far - - - - - ces!
Ком.
Com.
дай_те, дай_те, дай_те намъ ко - ме - - - - - дій!
du co - mi_que, de la co - mé - di - - - - - - e!
Траг.
Trag.
дай - те намъ тра - - ге - - - - - - - - дій!
de la tra - gé - - di - - - - - - - - e!
gen - - - - - - - - - - - - do
cresc.
ff

10
Poco più sostenuto (Allegro moderato).
Траг.
Trag.
Тра -
Du tra -
Десять Чудаковъ, раздвинувъ занавѣсъ посерединѣ, выбѣгаютъ на просценіумъ и гигантскими лопатами разгребаютъ дерущихся.
Dix Ridicules, écartant le rideau au milieu, se précipitent sur le proscenium et avec des pelles géantes débalayent la scène des combattants.
Ти - - - - - - - - - - - - ше! Ти - ше!
Eh! si - len - ce!
Poco più sostenuto (Allegro moderato).
10
V-ni e Fiat.
Bassi, Fag.
m.d.
Пустоголовые
Têtes Vides
Фар - совъ!
Des far - ces!
Комики
Les Comiques
Ко - ме - дій!
Du co - mi - que!
Траг.
Trag.
ге - дій!
gi - que!
Ра - зой - ди - - - тесь!
Quit-tez la scè - - - ne!
Сту-пай - те
Al - lez vous
Чуд.
Rid.
V-ni
m.d.

Лирики
Les Lyriques
Люб - ви!
L'a - mour!
Чуд.
Rid.
въ залъ!
en!
Сту - пай-те на га -
Al - lez dans la
m.d.
11
лер - - - - - ку!
sal - - - - - le!
V-ni
Cor.

Чудаки сгребаютъ лопатами ссорящихся въ обѣ кулисы.
Les Ridicules ramassent avec les pelles les combattants, les refoulant dans les coulisses.
Чуд.
Rid.
Мы вамъ пред ста - - - - вимъ!
Vo - yez notre spec ta - - - - - cle!
Fl.
scherzando
fp
8
Мы вамъ по ка жемъ!
C'est du bon thé â - - tre!
Э - то на сто
C'est in com pa
mp
12
я ще е!
ra - ble!
Э - - то без по доб - но е!
C'est là qu'est le vrai che min!
Quart.
mp

Въ упоенiи.
Enthousiasmés.
Любовь къ тремъ апельсинамъ!
L'amour pour trois Oranges!
Любовь къ тремъ апельсинамъ!
L'amour pour trois Oranges!
Чуд.
Rid.
Ob.
13
Разогнавъ толпу, Чудаки влѣзаютъ въ башни, тенора въ одну, басы въ другую.
Ayant chassé la foule, les Ridicules montent dans les tours, les ténors dans l'une, les basses dans l'autre.
Смотрите!
Silence!
Слушайте!
Chut, silence!
Смот-
Du
cresc.
14
Слушайте!
Pas de bruit!
рите!
calme!
V-ni, spic.
T-be
8va bassa

Кричатъ изъ башенъ по направленію къ сценѣ.
Ils crient des tours dans la direction de la scène.
Чуд.
Rid.
За - на-вѣсъ!
Vite, ri-deau!
Да - вай - те
Et qu'on com
за - - - - - на -
men - - - - - - - -
ff
Quart.
f
вѣсъ!
ce!
mf cresc.
Занавѣсъ посерединѣ немного раздвигается и пропускаетъ глашатая съ трубачемъ.
Le rideau s'ouvrant un peu au milieu laisse passer un hêraut avec un trompette.
15
Трубачъ, трубитъ въ басовый тромбонъ.
LeTrompette, joue le signal sur une trombone basse.
sempre ff
ff

T-ne basso
f
dim.
sf
T-ne basso
sf
sf
16
T-ne basso
f
Celli e Fag.
pp
T-ne basso
pp

17
Глашатай, внушительно.
Le Héraut, d'une manière imposante.
Ко - роль Трефъ
Le Roi de Trè - - - - - fles
Глаш.
Hér.
въ от - - - - ча - - - я -
est au dé - ses -
ньи,
poir,
18
по - - - то - - му что
car son fils,

Глаш.
Hér.
сынъ
e -
en - fant
ché -
f
pp
го,
ri
19
на -
et
mp
слѣд - ный принцъ,
prince hé - ri - tier,
Tutti
ff
бо - ленъ
souf - fre

20
Глаш.
Hér.
и
d'une
pp
по - хон - дри - че - ской бо - лѣз - нью.
hy - po - con - dri - e in - cu - ra - ble.
21
mp
8

Трубачъ
Le Trompette
ff
ff Tutti
p
T-ne basso
V-ni
p
dolce
22
Уходятъ.
Sortent.
pizz. e Cl. bas.
pp
8va bassa
Чудаки, съ радостнымъ волненіемъ.
Les Ridicules, avec une agitation joyeuse.
Tenori
На-чи-на- - ет-
Ça com-men- - - -
mf
8va bassa

Чуд.
Rid.
ся!
ce!
На - чи -
Ça com -
На - чи - на - - ет - - ся!
Ça com - men - - - - - ce!
8va bassa
23
на - ет - - ся!
men - - - ce!
На - - - - - - чи - - - - - -
Ça com - - - - -
pp
cresc.
8va bassa
ff
на - - - - - - - - - - - - - ет - ся!
men - - - - - - - - - - - - - ce!
f
dim.
p
8va bassa
24
Занавѣсъ медленно поднимается.
Le rideau se lève lentement.
T-be
f
ff
fff
Attacca

АКТЪ I. / ACTE I.

КАРТИНА I. / TABLEAU I.

Королевскій дворецъ. Король. Рядомъ съ нимъ Панталонъ. Передъ ними медики съ медицинскими инструментами.

Le palais du Roi. Le Roi. Près de lui Pantalon. Devant eux des médecins avec des instruments médicaux.

Мед.
Méd.
бо-ли въ вискахъ, раз - ли-ті-е жел-чи, не-сва-ре-ні-е же - луд-ка, сильна-я от-
des maux de tê - te, une a-pep-si - e, la faibles-se des ar - tères, la tê - te ra-mol -
Ob., Cl.
p
28
рыж-ка, му - чи - тель-ный ка-шель, от - сут-ствi - е сна, от - сут-ствi - е
li - e, une toux dou-lou - reu - se, la vue af - fai - blie, un corps a - né -
Fag.
Король, въ ужасѣ.
Le Roi, terrifié.
До - воль - но!
Que fai - re?
ап-пе-ти-та, серд-це-бі - е-ні - е, го-ло - во-кру - же-ні - е, часты-е
mique et maigre, bien trop de bi - le, des é - tour - dis - se - ments, des ter-reurs sans mo -
Ob., Ob. c-a., Cl.
mf

29
Король.
Roi.
До-воль - но!
Que fai - re?
Мед.
Méd.
об - мо-ро-ки,
tifs é-vi-dents,
мрач-ны - я мыс-ли,
de longues syn-co-pes,
не-хо-ро-ші - я пред
de mauvais pres-sen-ti
- чув-стві-я, рав-но -
- ments, une in-dif-fé -
p
Ob. c.-a.
ду-ші-е къ жиз-ни,
ren-ce pour tout, des
пол - на-я а
peurs i-nex-pli
- па-ті-я,
- ca - bles,
30
ост-ра-я ме-лан
et la mé-lan-co
- хо-лі-я, о-
- lie pro-fon-de,
f
V. I
mf
Ob. Cl.
pizz.
Король, затыкая уши.
Le Roi, se bouchant les oreilles.
До - воль - но!
Mi - sè - re!
До - воль - - но!
Mi - sè - - re!
пас-на-я ме-лан
et la mé-lan-co
- хо-лі-я,
- lie noi-re,
чер-на-я ме-лан
et la mé-lan-co
- хо-лі-я:
- lie ai-gue:

Poco più mosso.

31

Вѣско, дѣлая заключеніе.

Faisant avec importance la conclusion.

Мед.
Méd.

не - пре - о - до - ли - мо - е и - по - хон -
un é - tat d'hy - po - con - drie que nous ju -

Poco più mosso.

31

Fiati

Король
Le Roi

Какъ? какъ?
Quoi? quoi?

Мед.
Méd.

дри - че - ско - е яв - ле - ні - е.
geons in - gué - ris - sa - ble.

32

Мед.
Méd.

Не - пре - о - до - ли - мо - е и - по - хон - дри - че - ско - е яв -
Un é - tat d'hy - po - con - drie que nous ju - geons in - gué - ris -

32

Король
Le Roi
pp
33
rit.
И что жъ?
Et bien?
Мед.
Méd.
ле - ні - е.
sa - ble.
Без - на - деж - но.
In - cu - ra - ble.
T-be, T-ni e Piatti
f
pp T-ni
pp rit.
Панталонъ
Pantalon
34 Poco meno mosso.
f assai rit.
Король трагическимъ движеніемъ руки отпускаетъ медиковъ, которые уходятъ, забравъ свои инструменты.
Le Roi renvoie par un mouvement tragique de la main les médecins, qui s'en vont emportant leurs instruments.
Бѣд - ный Принцъ!
Pau - vre Prince!
Бѣд - ный Принцъ!
Pau - vre Prince!
Въ отчаяньи.
Avec désespoir.
Бѣд - ный Принцъ!
Pau - vre fils!
Бѣд - ный, бѣд - ный сынъ!
Mon mal - heu - reux en - fant!
34 Poco meno mosso.
Celli
f molto espress.
V. I
f espress.
m.s.
assai rit.
p
35 Andante.
Съ ужасомъ повторяютъ приговоръ медиковъ.
Terrifiés, répètent la conclusion des médecins.
Пант.
Pant.
Не - пре - о - до - ли - мо - е...
Les doc - teurs ont con - sta - té...
Король.
Roi.
Не - пре - о - до - ли - мо - е...
Les doc - teurs ont con - sta - té...
35 Andante.
V-ni sul pontic.
pp
Fl.
Cl. bas.

36
Пант.
Pant.
и‿по‿хон‿дри‿че‿ско‿е...
un é‿tat d'hy‿po‿condri‿e...
Король.
Roi.
и‿по‿хон‿дри‿че‿ско‿е...
un é‿tat d'hy‿po‿condri‿e...
pp
pp
Fl.
pp
pizz.
яв‿ле‿ні‿е...
in‿cu‿ra‿ble...
Король падаетъ въ кресло.
Le Roi tombe dans le fauteuil.
яв‿ле‿ні‿е...
in‿cu‿ra‿ble...
poco rit.
T-be con sord.
37 Poco meno mosso.
Горячо.
Vivement.
Ахъ, эти негодные
Ah! grand Dieu, c'est ça la méde‿
Скорбно повторяетъ болѣзни сына.
Répétant tristement les maladies de son fils.
Бо‿ли въ пе‿че‿ни, бо‿ли въ поч‿кахъ, бо‿ли въ за‿тыл‿кѣ,
Des dou‿leurs au foie, des dou‿leurs au reins, des maux de tê‿te,
Cl. e Cl. bas.
pizz. e Timp.

Пант.
Pant.
ме-ди-ки! Ни-че-го о-ни не зна-ютъ, ни-че-го не мо-гутъ выле-чить!
ci - ne! Ils ne savent rien de rien, ils ne peuvent rien gué-rir!
Король.
Roi.
бо-ли въ вис-кахъ, раз-ли-ті-е жел-чи, не-сва-ре-ні-е же-луд-ка,
l'in-di-ges-tion, des trou-bles ner-veux, — la faib-les-se des ar-tères, de
pp
38
Передразнивая медиковъ.
Contrefaisant les médecins.
„Бо-ли въ пе-че-ни!“ Долж-ны вы-ле-чить бо-ли въ пе-че-ни!
Il a mal au foie! Que dia-ble, soi-gnez lui donc le foie!
серд-це-бі-е-ні-е, го-ло-во-кру-же-ні-е,
l'asth-me chro-ni-que, une toux dou-lou-reuse, des syn-
Ob. c-al.
p
„Бо-ли въ поч-кахъ!“ Долж-ны вы-ле-чить бо-ли въ поч-кахъ!
Il a mal aux reins! Que dia-ble, soi-gnez lui donc les reins!
ча-сты-е об-мо-ро-ки, мрач-ны-я мыс-ли...
co-pes pro-fon-des et la vue af-fai-bli-e...

39 Più animato.
Встaвая.
Se levant.
Король.
Roi.
А я ужъ старъ! Ко - му же перейдетъ мо - е цар_ство?
Je suis si vieux! Qui donc hé_ri_te_ra de mon ro_yau_me?
V. I
Celli
f espress.
fp
f
40 Poco più animato.
Не - у - же - ли пле - мян - ни - цѣ Кла -
Se - rait ce ma niè - ce Cla -
Celli
Bassi
ри - че? Чу - дач - кѣ? Же_сто - кой жен - щинѣ?
ri - ce? Si cru_el - le et ri - di - cu - le?
V-le
41 Pochissimo meno.
Панталонъ
Pantalon
Бѣд - ный! Бѣд - ный!
Pau - vre! Pau - vre!
Съ рыданiями.
Sanglotant.
О, бѣд - ный я! О, бѣд - ный сынъ!
O, pau - vre moi! O, pau - vre fils!
41 Pochissimo meno.
V. I e Ob.
Cor.

Рыдаетъ, прильнувъ къ королевской мантіи.
Sanglote dans le manteau du Roi.
Пант.
Pant.
Бѣд - но - е!
Pau - vre!
Король рыдаетъ.
Le Roi sanglote.
Король.
Roi.
Бѣд - но - е цар - ство!
Pau - vre ro - yau - me!
Allegro.
Чудаки, которые все время съ волненіемъ слѣдили за Королемъ, боясь, что Король оскандалится передъ публикой.
Les Ridicules, suivent tout le temps avec inquiétude la conduite du Roi, craignant qu'il ne se soit rendu grotesque par devant le public.
42
Онъ за-бы-ва-етъ свое ве-ли-чі-е!
Mais il perdra son prestige ro-yal!
За-бы-ва-етъ!
Son pres-ti-ge...
Allegro.
Ве-ли-чі-е!
Nous sommes choqués!
pizz. e Fiati
Andante.
Панталонъ, успокаивая Короля.
Pantalon, calmant le Roi.
43
Пант.
Pant.
Не па-до...
Calmez vous...
Не па-до...
Cal-mez vous...
Andante.
V-ni con sord.
dolce
Celli, Bas., Fag.
espr.

Стихнувъ, мечтательно.
Se calmant et comme en rêve.
44
Король.
Roi.
Од-на-жды док-то-ра ска-за-ли, что
Ja-dis les doc-teurs ont dit que
Ped.
p dolce
толь-ко смѣхъ быть мо-жетъ вы-ле-чить е-го...
seul le ri-re pou-vait gué-rir mon pau-vre fils...
Ob., Cor.
Più mosso.
Панталонъ, убѣжденно.
Pantalon, d'un ton convaincu.
45
Andante.
Такъ на-до, чтобъ онъ смѣ-ял-ся!
A-lors qu'on le fas-se ri-re!
Без-на-деж-но.
Fai-ble chan-ce.
Celli
f energico
V. I
pp

46 Allegro.
Все болѣе и болѣе оживляясь.
De plus en plus agité.
Пант.
Pant.
Не-об-хо-ди-мо, чтобъ онъ смѣ-ял-ся!
Il faut le fai-re ri-re quand mê-me!
Король.
Roi.
46 Allegro.
Fag. e pizz.
mf
Fl.
p
Cl.
Fl.
За-чѣмъ нашъ дворъ въ пе-ча-ли? За-чѣмъ всѣ хо-дятъ, какъ
La cour est bien trop tris-te. Les gens se trai-nent, les
Cl.
Ob.
47
V-ni
pp
въ во-ду о-пу-щен-ны-е? Вѣдь такъ нашъ Принцъ ни-ког-да не за-смѣ-
tê-tes bais-sées et mor-nes. Com-ment vou-lez vous que le Prin-ce puis-se
pp
ет-ся. На-до, чтобъ бы-ло ве-се-ло во-кругъ.
ri-re? Tout, tout doit ê-tre gai au-tour de lui.
mf
f
p
T-ni
f

48 Più mosso.
Открывъ путь для исцѣленія Принца; радостно.
Ayant trouvé le moyen de guérir le Prince; avec joie.
Пант.
Pant.
Объ - я - вить бы празд - ни - ки, у - стро - ить
Король
Le Roi
J'ai trou - vé ce qu'il faut pour é - ga - yer le
Ни - ког - да бѣд - ный
Non, ja - mais le pau - vre
48 Più mosso.
V. I, Fl.
pp
иг - ры, ма - ска - ра - ды, ра - зыг - рать бле - стя - щі - е спек -
Prin - ce: qu'on or - don - ne des spec - ta - cles, des tour - nois, des
Король.
Roi.
Принцъ не за - смѣ - ет - - - ся!
Prin - ce ne ri - ra!
pp
так - ли, до - стать лю - дей, у - мѣ - ю - щихъ смѣ - шить.
fêtes, qu'on ap - pelle des gens qui peuvent le fai - re rire.
Панталонъ, вспомнивъ нужное имя, кричитъ благимъ матомъ въ кулису.
Pantalon, se rappelant du nom dont il a besoin, crie à tue tête dans la coulisse.
49
ff
Труф - фаль - ди - - - - - - но!!
Trouf - fal - di - - - - - - no!!
ff Tutti
Cor.

ff
Пант.
Pant.
Труф-фаль - ди - - - но!!
Trouf-fal - di - - - no!!
ff
Cor.
ff
ff
50
Труффаль - ди - но!
Trouf-fal - di - no!
Король
Le Roi
Иг - ры? Спек - так-ли?
Des fê - tes? Des spec-ta-cles?
50
pp pizz. e Cl.
pp
51
Махнувъ рукой.
Faisant avec la main
un signe désespéré.
По - мо-жетъ и - ли нѣтъ,
Pour-quoi ne pas le faire,
Король.
Roi.
Не по - мо - жетъ...
I - nu - ti - le!
51
V. I
fp
V-le pizz.
намъ на - доб - но ис - про - бо - вать.
si ça pou - vait sau - ver le Prince.

Кричитъ въ кулису.
Criant vers la coulisse.
Пант.
Pant.
Труф - фаль - ди - но!!
Trouf - fal - di - no!!
pizz. e Cor.
tutti
52
Труффальдино, вбѣгаетъ опрометью, и прямо къ Панталону.
Trouffaldino, se précipite en courant vers Pantalon.
За - чѣмъ те - бѣ я ну - женъ?
En quoi te suis-je u - ti - le?
V-ni e Cl.
T-be, Cor.
colla parte
Cor.
Панталонъ, важно.
Pantalon, avec importance.
Ты ну - женъ Ко - ро - лю.
Pas à moi, à ton Roi.
53
Fl. e Quart.
m.d.
Cor.
54
Труффальдино кидается къ Королю, и прямо на колѣни.
Trouffaldino se précipite à genoux devant le Roi.
Quart.
Fiati.

V. I
ff
p
Ped.
55
Король, задумчиво.
Le Roi, pensif.
Вотъ что, Труф - фаль - -
Dis moi, Trouf - fal - -
p Arpe e Quart.
Ped.
Король.
Roi.
ди - - - - - но: я хо - -
di - - - - - no: je vou - -
p
Ped.
56
Король.
Roi.
чу у - стро - - - ить
drais don - - ner des
Ped.

Кор.
Roi.
празд - - - - - - - - - ни - - ки
fê - - - - - - - - - - - - tes
57
и по - пы - тать - ся раз - смѣ - - -
pour es - sa - yer de fai - re
шить на - - - - - ше - го
rire le pau - vre
Прин - - - - - ца...
Prin - - - - - ce...
p
mf
pp
Ped.

58
Труффальдино, скороговоркой.
Trouffaldino, ayant à peine le temps de prononcer toutes les paroles.
Убѣгаетъ.
Il sort en courant.
Все будетъ сдѣлано.
Tout se_ra fait de suite.
Самы_е ве_се_лы_е праздники.
Ça y est! Je vais ar_ranger des fêtes.
colla parte

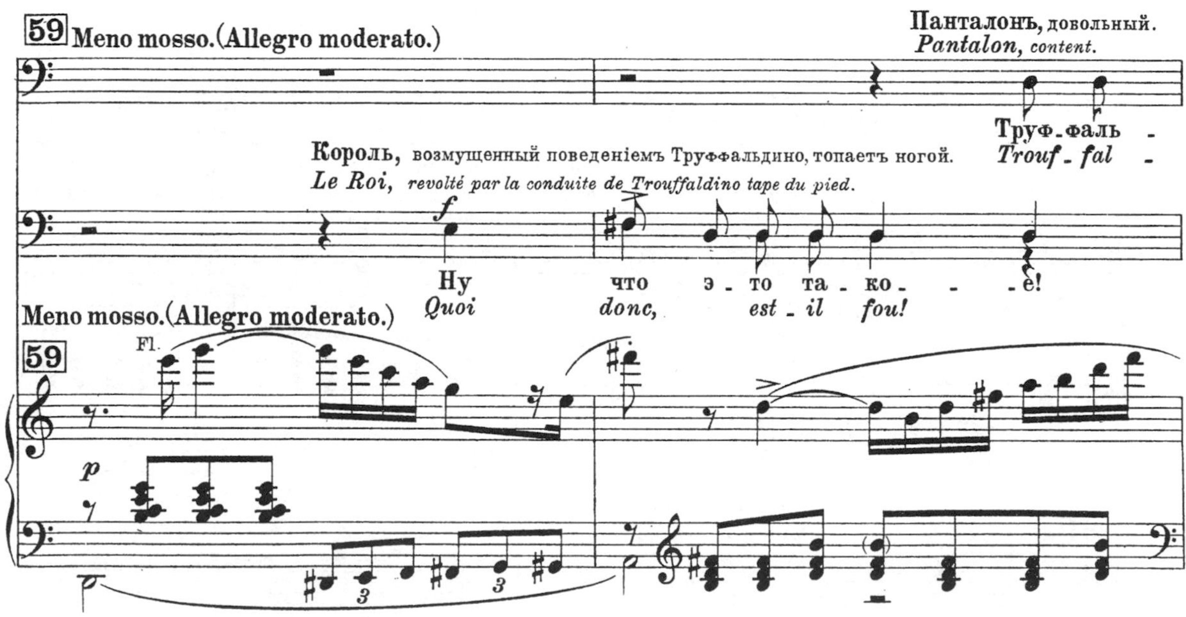

59 Meno mosso. (Allegro moderato.)
Панталонъ, довольный.
Pantalon, content.
Труф_фаль -
Trouf_fal -
Король, возмущенный поведеніемъ Труффальдино, топаетъ ногой.
Le Roi, revolté par la conduite de Trouffaldino tape du pied.
Ну что э_то та_ко_ _ _е!
Quoi donc, est_il fou!
Meno mosso. (Allegro moderato.)
59
Fl.

Король ударяетъ въ ладоши.
Le Roi frappe dans les mains.
Пант.
Pant.
ди_ _ _но, э_то хо_ро_шо!
di_ _ _no, c'est vraiment parfait.
mp cresc. e un poco rit.

60 Poco meno mosso.
Про себя. A part.
Пант.
Pant.
Э - то хо - ро - шо.
O oui, c'est très bien.
Король, вошедшимъ слугамъ.
Le Roi, aux serviteurs qui viennent d'entrer.
При - гла - сить къ намъ Ле - ан - дра,
Nous vou - lons voir Lé - an - dre,
Poco meno mosso.
60
pesante
Cor. e Quart.
Король.
Roi.
на - ше - го пер - ва - го ми - нист - ра.
no - tre pre - mier mi - nis - tre.
Fl., Cl.
61
Панталонъ, тихо и гнѣвно.
Pantalon, tout bas, en colère.
Ой, Ле - андръ... онъ хо - четъ зла...
Ah, Lé - andre... je le dé - teste.
Cor. c. sord.
pizz. e Cl.
Celli
fp ben tenuto
Пант.
Pant.
Онъ хо - четъ смер - ти Прин - ца...
Il veut la mort du Prin - ce.
ritenuto

Входитъ Леандръ и отвѣшиваетъ низкій поклонъ по этикету.
Entre Léandre qui salue profondément selon l'étiquette.
62
Andante.
Король
Le Roi
Ле_андръ, объ_я_вить не_
Lé_andre, qu'on or_donne de
pp ben tenuto
Король. Roi.
медлен_но ве_се_лы_е иг_ры и празд_ни_ки,
sui - te des fê_tes jo_yeu_ses, des ga_las su_perbes,
Чудаки, очень довольные приказомъ Короля, повторяютъ за нимъ.
Les Ridicules, très contents de l'ordre du Roi, répètent après lui.
Празд_ни_ки!
Ga_las su_perbes!
Иг_ры!
Fê_tes!
Король. Roi.
хит_ры_е спек_так_ли, на_ряд_ны_е ма_ска_ра_ды.
qu'on pré_pare des lut_tes, de fol_les mas_ca_ra_des.
Спек_так_ли!
Des lut_tes!
Чуд. Rid.
cresc.
mp

63 Allegro moderato.
Чуд.
Rid.
Ма - ска-ра-ды, ма - ска-ра-ды, ма - ска-ра - довъ ма - - ло!
Mas - ca-ra-des, mas - ca-ra-des, mas - ca-ra-des, c'est mai - - gre!
63 Allegro moderato.
Fiati
V-ni
Леандръ, Королю.
Léandre, au Roi.
О, Ко-роль, не за - смѣ - ет-ся нашъ боль -
Oh, mon Roi, ça fa - tigue - ra le pau-vre
Чуд.
Rid.
Il
На - до вак - ха - на - лій! Вак - ха -
faut des bac - cha - na - les! Bac - cha -
64
Леан.
Léan.
ной.
Prince.
Чуд.
Rid.
на - лій, вак - ха - на - лій, вак - ха - на - - - - - -
na - les, bac - cha - na - les, bac - cha - na - - - - - -
64

Панталонъ, сердито.
Pantalon, en colère.

Ахъ!
Ah!

Леан.
Léan.

По - мочь не мо - жетъ все э - - - - то.
Ce - la est bien i - nu - ti - - - - - le.

Чуд.
Rid.

- - - лій!
- - - les!

f

Cl. bas. 1
mp

65

Король
Le Roi

Все жъ намъ на - доб - но ис - про - бо - вать.
Il faut tou - jours ten - ter la chan - ce.

Fiati
p

Fl.

Des

Приказывая.
En ordonnant.

Король.
Roi.

Подчеркивая.
Soulignant.

Иг - - - ры, празд - ни - ки и вак - ха -
jeux, des spec - ta - - cles, des bac - cha -

ten.

p

66
Леандръ, съ трудомъ скрывая гнѣвъ.
Léandre, cachant à peine sa colère.
a piacere
Шумъ по.вре.дитъ е - го здо.ро.вью!
Il en se - ra bien plus ma.la - de!
Уходя, безпрекословно.
S'en allant ordonne avec autorité.
Король.
Roi.
на - лі.и!
na - les!
Празд - ни - ки
Des fê - tes,
Чудаки, довольные.
Les Ridicules, contents.
А!
Ah!
66
T-be con sord.
Fiati
p
f colla parte
f
p
Панталонъ, Леандру, съ бѣшенствомъ.
Pantalon, à Léandre, avec rage.
67
Слѣдуетъ за Королемъ.
Suit le Roi.
ff
Пре - да - тель!!
Ah, traî - tre!!
Леан.
Léan.
Фиг.ляръ!
Bouf.fon!
Уходитъ.
Sort.
Король
Roi.
и вак.ха - на - лі - и.
des bac.cha - na - les.
67
Quart. sul pontic.
p
f
ff
mf
f
T-be e Cor. con sord.
Attacca.

КАРТИНА II.

Темнѣетъ, и опускается кабалистическій занавѣсъ, который оставляетъ для дѣйствія только небольшую часть сцены. Вся картина протекаетъ въ темнотѣ.

TABLEAU II.

La scène devient sombre. Un rideau cabalistique descent, laissant seulement une petite partie de la scène pour l'action. Tout le tableau se joue dans l'obscurité.

Чудаки, пораженные.
Ridicules, bouleversés.
Магъ Че_лій!
C'est Tché_lio!
Огонь и дымъ въ другомъ мѣстѣ, рядомъ съ Магомъ Челіемъ.
Le feu et la fumée apparaissent à une autre place de la scène, près du Magicien Tchélio.
T-be e pizz.
fp
p
cresc.
72
Съ громомъ и молніей Фата Моргана.
Fata Morgana apparait avec tonnerres et éclairs.
V-ni
T-be
fff
T-ni
Чудаки, еще болѣе удивленные.
Les Ridicules, encore plus bouleversés.
Фа_та Мор_га_на!
Fa_ta Mor_ga_na!
T-ni, Cor., Timp.
ff
T-be e pizz.
fp

Сцена кишитъ чертенятами. Они приносятъ столъ, который ставятъ между Челіемъ и Фатой, игральныя карты и огромныя изображенія короля Трефъ и короля Пикъ, которыя помѣщаютъ, первое позади Челія, второе позади Фаты. Оба изображенія свѣтятся въ темнотѣ.

La scène pululle de petits diables. Ils apportent une table qu'ils placent entre Tchélio et Fata, des cartes et des immenses tableaux du roi de Trèfles et du roi de Piques qu'ils posent le premier derrière Tchélio et le second derrière Fata. Les deux tableaux sont lumineux et brillent dans l'obscurité.

Черт.
Diab.
И!
Hi!
mp
p
75
Чудаки
Les Ridicules
Иг - ра - ютъ въ кар
Ils jouent aux car
76
f
Чуд.
Rid.
ты.
tes.
Игра начинается. Челій сдаетъ карты преувеличеннаго размѣра. Чертенята пускаются въ адскій плясъ, образуя хороводъ вокругъ играющихъ Челія и Фаты.
Le jeu commence. Tchélio donne les cartes qui sont d'une dimension exagérée. Les petits diables commencent une danse infernale faisant une ronde autour de Tchélio et de Fata Morgana.
V-ni, Ob., Fl., Picc.

Черт.
Diab.
И!
Hi!
77
Фата ходитъ.
Fata joue.
Челій ходитъ.
Tchélio joue.
T-be, T-ni, Timp.

78

Фата Моргана, выигравъ, торжествующе.
Fata Morgana, ayant gagné, triomphante.

f *ff*

Ха!
Ha!

Челій, проигравъ, яростно.
Tchélio, ayant perdu, avec rage.

f *ff*

О!
Oh!

Черт.
Diab.

ff

Чертенята падаютъ на колѣни.
Les petits diables tombent à genoux.

Чертенята падаютъ ницъ.
Les petits diables se prosternent.

И!
Hi!

78 Фата ходитъ.
Fata joue.

ff

Чудаки
Ridicules

Изображеніе короля Трефъ блекнетъ. Изображеніе короля Пикъ становится ярче.
L'image du roi de Trèfles s'obscurcit. L'image du roi de Piques devient plus lumineuse.

Бѣд - ный Ко - роль!
Oh! pau - vre Roi!

Сча - стье съ Ле - ан - дромъ!
La chance est à Lé - an - dre!

etc.

V-le

p subito

senza cresc.

79 Чертенята
Les petits diables

Сдаетъ Фата Моргана. Чертенята вскакиваютъ и пускаются въ адскій плясъ.
Fata Morgana donne les cartes. Les petits diables se lèvent brusquement et commencent une ronde infernale.

f

И!
Hi!

И!
Hi!

V.I, Ob., Fl., Picc.

f subito

ff *f*

Черт.
Diab.

И!
Hi!

5 5 5 5

f

Черт.
Diab.

И!
Hi!

11 11

ff

Черт.
Diab.

80

f

И!
Hi!

f

И!
Hi!

11 11

ff

Челій ходитъ.
Tchélio joue.

T-be, T-ni, Timp., V-ni

Фата ходитъ.
Fata joue.

Челій ходитъ.
Tchélio joue.

Челій, опять проигравъ, яростно.
Tchélio, perdant de nouveau, avec fureur.

81

f

ff

О!
Oh!

Черт.
Diab.

f

И!
Hi!

f

И!
Hi!

ff

И!
Hi!

Чертенята падаютъ на колѣни.
Les petits diables tombent à genoux.

Фата ходитъ.
Fata joue.

Челій ходитъ.
Tchelio joue.

Фата ходитъ.
Fata joue.

Челій ходитъ.
Tchélio joue.

81

Фата ходитъ.
Fata joue.

ff

Фата Моргана, торжествующе.
Fata Morgana, victorieusement.

Изображеніе короля Трефъ еще болѣе меркнетъ. Король Пикъ дѣлается ярче.
L'image du roi de Trèfles s'obscurcit encore plus. L'image du roi de Piques devient encore plus lumineuse.

f *ff*

Ха!
Ha!

Чудаки
Les Ridicules

Чертенята падаютъ ницъ.
Les petits diables se prosternent.

О - пять Ле - андръ!
En - core Lé - andre!

Бѣд - ный Ко-
Oh, pau - vre

V-le

p subito

senza cresc.

Чертенята
Les petits diables

82

И!
Hi!

роль!
Roi!

Сдаетъ Магъ Челій. Чертенята пускаются въ плясъ, болѣе бѣшенный, чѣмъ предыдущій.
Le Magicien Tchélio donne les cartes. Les petits diables commencent une danse encore plus endiablée.

Чуд.
Rid.

82

f subito

Черт.
Diab.

И!
Hi!

83

f

И!
Hi!

8

f

cresc.

Фата ходитъ.
Fata joue.

Челій ходитъ.
Tchélio joue.

ff

Черт.
Diab.
И! И! И! И! И!
Hi! Hi! Hi! Hi! Hi!

Фата Fata Челій Tchélio
Фата Fata Челій Tchélio
Фата Fata Челій Tchélio
Фата Fata Челій Tchélio
Фата Fata Челій Tchélio

Фата Моргана поднимаетъ высоко въ воздухѣ послѣднюю карту.
Fata Morgana lève la dernière carte au dessus de sa tête.

84

Черт.
Diab.
И! И! И! И!
Hi! Hi! Hi! Hi!

Фата Fata Челій Tchélio
Фата Fata Челій Tchélio

Ходитъ съ нея.
Fata joue la carte.

Фата Моргана, хохочетъ торжествующимъ сатанинскимъ смѣхомъ.
***Fata Morgana**, d'un rire satanique et victorieux.*

Ха-ха-ха-ха! Ха-ха-ха-ха! Ха-ха-ха-ха!
Ha-ha-ha-ha! Ha-ha-ha-ha! Ha-ha-ha-ha!

Челій, окончательно проигравъ, потрясаетъ руками.
***Tchélio**, perdant définitivement agite les bras avec rage.*

Про-кля-та-я! Про-кля-та-я! Про-кля-та-я! Про-
Mau-di-te! Sois mau-di-te! Sois mau-di-te! Sois mau-

Черт.
Diab.
Подобострастно.
Servilement.

Фа-та Мор-га-на, Фа-та Мор-га-на, Фа-та Мор-га-на,
Fa-ta Mor-ga-na, Fa-ta Mor-ga-na, Fa-ta Mor-ga-na,

T-be c. sord. e Quart. col legno

85
Фата.
Fata.
Ха - ха - ха - ха!
Ha - ha - ha - ha!
Ха - ха - ха - ха - ха - ха - ха!
Ha - ha - ha - ha - ha - ha - ha!
Чел.
Tchél.
кля - та - я! Про - кля - - - - та - я!
di - te! Sois mau di - - - - - - te!
Черт.
Diab.
Фа - та Мор - га - на, Фа - та Мор - га - - на!
Fa - ta Mor - ga - na, Fa - ta Mor - ga - - na!
85
Cl. e V.I
m.d.
m.s.
Фата Моргана
Fata Morgana
Ле - - - андръ!
Lé - - - an - - dre!
Челій
Tchélio
Сгиб - - - ни!
Crè - - - ve!
Чертенята
Les petits diables
И!
Hi!
Cor. e T-be con sord.

Фата Моргана проваливается, обнимая сіяющее изображеніе короля Пикъ.
Fata Morgana s'enfonce dans la terre tenant dans ses bras l'image lumineuse du roi de Piques.

КАРТИНА III.

Декорація первой картины. Леандръ одинъ на томъ же мѣстѣ, гдѣ находился.

TABLEAU III.

Décor du 1er tableau. Léandre est seule a la même place où il était.

Клар.
Clar.
Принцъ у - мретъ и я сдѣ - ла-юсь на-слѣд-ни-цей пре-сто - ла,
Prin - ce meurt, je suis hé - ri-tière du trô - ne de mon on - cle,
mf
p
mf
91
Poco meno mosso.
я вый-ду за васъ за - мужъ и под-ни - му васъ до тро - на.
et si nous per-dons le Prin - ce, je vous é - pou-se, Lé-an - dre.
mp pizz.e Fiati
mf
За - пом-ни-ли ль вы э - то?
M'a - vez vous bien com-pri - se?
Леандръ низко кланяется.
Léandre s'incline profondément.
Леандръ
Léandre
Да, Принцес - са.
Oui, Prin-ces-se.
Cl.
p
Fag.
C.F.
92
Allegro moderato.
Такъ что же вы дѣ - ла - е - те для здо - ро - вья Прин-ца? Вѣдь
Com-ment pou-vez vous a - gir a - vec au-tant de cal - me? Je
V-ni
f
fp
p

Клар.
Clar.
assai rit.
онъ безъ кон_ца про_жи_ветъ со сво_ей и_по_хон_дри_че_ской бо_лѣз_нью!
crains qu'il vi_vra plus que nous no_nob_stant sa ma_la_die hy_po_con_dria_que.
f
rit.
93
Клар.
Clar.
Дѣйствовать съ та_ко_ю флег_мо_ю какъ вы,— нѣтъ, вы пра_во
a tempo
E_tre fleg_ma_ti_que lors_qu'il faut o_ser! Non, vous ê_tes
p pizz.
cresc.
Клар.
Clar.
f
не_до_стой_ны мо_ей ру_ки и тро_на!
in_di_gne et de ma main et du trô_ne!
f
94
Meno mosso.
Леандръ
Léandre
p
Я дѣй_ству_ю не_мно_го
So_yez un peu pa_tien_te.
f
p
pp
pizz., Fag. e C.F.

Allegro.

95 Злокачественнымъ шопотомъ, вытягивая шею по направленію къ уху Клариче.
Tendant le cou vers l'oreille de Clarice lui chuchote méchamment.

Чудаки почти вываливаются изъ башенъ, высовываясь, чтобы разслышать слова Леандра.
Les Ridicules tombent presque des tours en se penchant pour entendre les paroles de Léandre.

Клариче, недовѣрчиво.
Clarice, incrédule.
96
Вотъ какъ!
Pas pos_sible!
Леан.
Léan.
ан_ски_ми сти_ха_ми.
vers mar_té_li_ens.
Я ихъ за_пи_хи_ва_ю въ хлѣбъ,
C'est dans son pain que je les glisse,
Ob., Fag.
Cor. con sord.
я ихъ кро_шу въ е_го по_хлеб_ку,
c'est dans sa soupe que je les hâ_che.
Ob. Fag.
T-be con sord.
97
и онъ у_мретъ отъ и_по_хон_дри_ческихъ кош_ма_ровъ.
Et il mour_ra d'u_ne ma_la_die hy_po_con_dria_que.
Quart. sul pontic.
98
Трагики, врываются на просценіумъ.
Les Tragiques, se ruant sur le proscenium.
Poco meno mosso.
Тра_ге_дій! Тра_ге_дій! Вы_со_кихъ тра_
Don_nez nous, don_nez nous de grandes tra_gé_
Quart.

Выскакиваютъ изъ башенъ и лопатами выгребаютъ Трагиковъ.
Se précipitent de leurs tours et avec des pelles débalaient la scène des Tragiques.
99
Траг.
Trag.
ге - дій! Скор - би! Сте - на - ній! У - бійствъ! Стра -
di - es! Meur - tres! Souf-fran - ces! Dou - leurs! Des
Чудаки, хватаясь за голову.
Les Ridicules, se tenant la tête.
О - пять о - ни!
En - core ces types!
да - ю - щихъ от - цовъ! Проник-но - ве - ній въсущ - ность!
â - mes tor - tu - rées! Des so - lu - tions pro - fon - des!
Tutti
100
Чудаки вытѣсняютъ Трагиковъ за кулису.
Les Ridicules repoussent les Tragiques dans la coulisse.
Трагики неожиданнымъ усиліемъ вновь врываются на сцену.
Les Tragiques par un effort inattendu pénètrent de nouveau sur la scène.
Meno mosso.
Мі - ро - выхъ стра - да - ній!
Des souf - frances mon - dia - les!
T-ni

Allegro.
Чудаки выгоняютъ ихъ.
Les Ridicules les chassent.
101
f
f
Tuba, Bassi e G. Cas.
Чудаки, съ разсерженнымъ видомъ возвращаются въ башни.
Les Ridicules, rentrent dans les tours avec un air agacé.
У - то - ми - тель_но!
Ça fa_tigue vrai_ment!
Fl., Cl.
p tranquillo
Fag.
Moderato.
102
Клариче
Clarice
Нѣтъ, Ле - андръ, я со - мнѣ_ва_юсь въ вашихъ
Non, Lé - andre, vos plans me pa_raissent i - nef - fi -
Ob.
p
p
Клар.
Clar.
сред - - ствахъ. Тутъ на - до
ca - - ces. Il ne faut
m. s.
p
mf
p

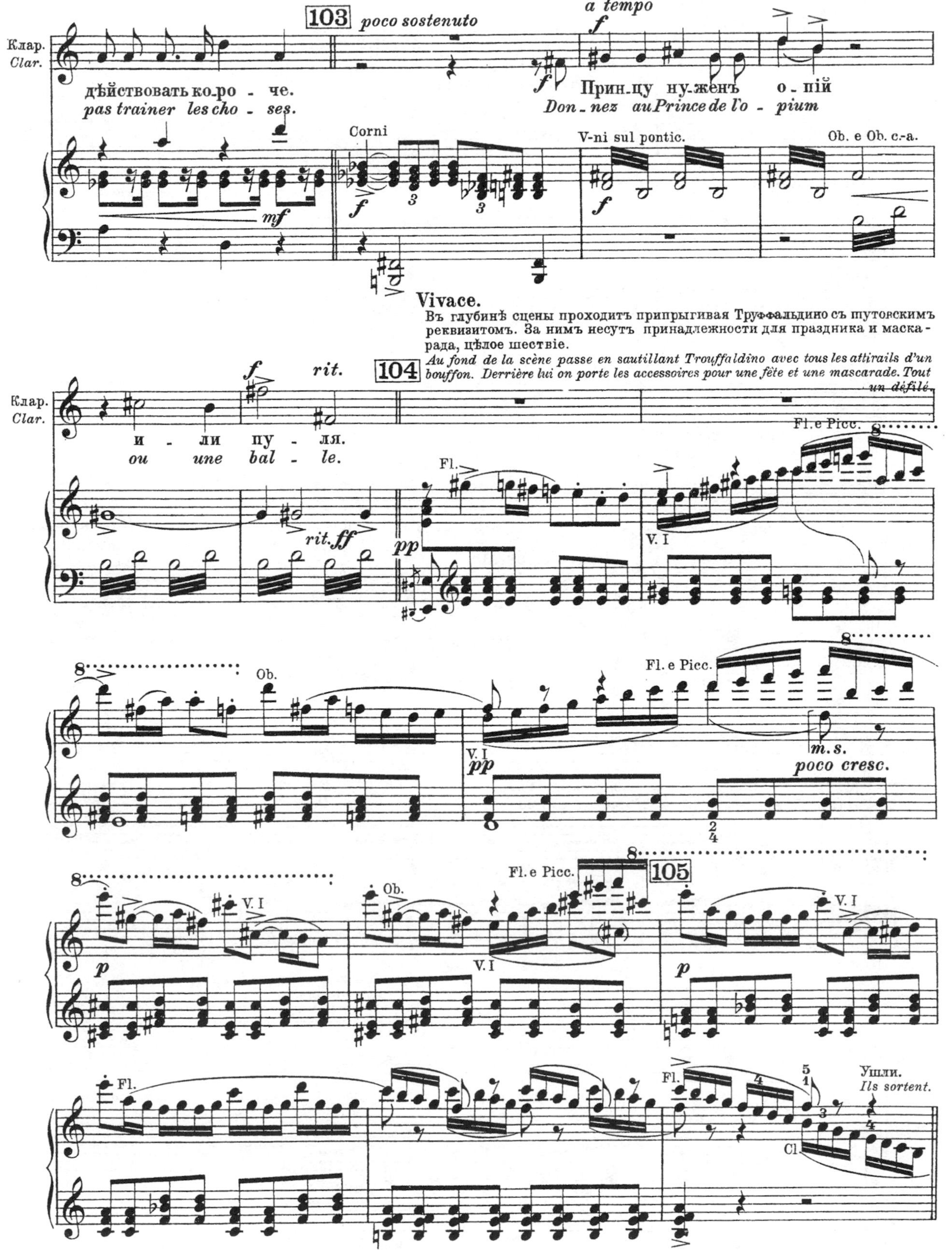
Клар.
Clar.
103 poco sostenuto
a tempo
дѣйствовать ко-ро - че.
pas trainer les cho - ses.
Прин-цу ну-женъ о-пій
Don-nez au Prince de l'o-pium
Corni
V-ni sul pontic.
Ob. e Ob. c.-a.
Vivace.
Въ глубинѣ сцены проходитъ припрыгивая Труффальдино съ шутовскимъ реквизитомъ. За нимъ несутъ принадлежности для праздника и маскарада, цѣлое шествіе.
Au fond de la scène passe en sautillant Trouffaldino avec tous les attirails d'un bouffon. Derrière lui on porte les accessoires pour une fête et une mascarade. Tout un défilé.
rit.
104
и - ли пу - ля.
ou une bal - le.
rit.
Fl.
Fl. e Picc.
V. I
Ob.
m.s.
poco cresc.
105
Cl.
Ушли.
Ils sortent.

106
Andante.
Клариче
Clarice
Кто э_тотъ че_ловѣкъ?
Qui est_ce? di_tes moi.
Леандръ
Léandre
Труффаль_ди_но, шутлива_я личность.
Trouffal _ di_no, un homme qui fait ri_re.
106 Andante.
T-ba c. sord.
pp
p
p
107 Allegro moderato.
Клар.
Clar.
Зачѣмъ онъ здѣсь?
Pourquoi vient-il?
Леан.
Léan.
Е _ го позвалъ Ко _ роль, чтобъ смѣ _
Le Roi l'a fait ve _ nir pour faire
107
Allegro moderato.
Cl.
p
p
Fag.
Леан.
Léan.
шить боль _ _ но _ го. На зав _ тра на _
rire le Prin _ ce. Dès de _ main on donne _
p
pizz.
Гнѣвно потрясаетъ рукою въ ту сторону, гдѣ скрылся Труффальдино.
Léandre d'un geste coléreux agite le bras dans la direction où est disparu Trouffaldino.
108
Леан.
Léan.
f
зна _ че _ ны празд _ нества, и э _ тотъ че _ ло _
ra de gran_des fê _ _ tes, et ce po _ li _ chi _
f

Саркастически.
Sarcastique.
Леан.
Léan.
вѣкъ будетъ ходить на голо-вѣ, лишь бы
nelle va pi-rouet-ter même sur la tête pour-vu que le
f Quart, T-be, T-ne
f
109 Molto animato.
Леан.
Léan.
Принцъ смѣ-ял-ся!
Prince ri-go-le!
p giocoso
Чудаки, весело и задорно.
Les Ridicules, gaîment et avec verve.
f
Принцъ ис-цѣ-лит-ся, ког-да онъ за-смѣ-
Il va gué-rir quand on pour-ra le fai-re
f
ет-ся.
ri-re.
p
Всѣ за-смѣ-ют-ся, ког-
On va bien rire quand on sau-
Чуд.
Rid.
p
pp

110
Чуд.
Rid.
да онъ ис - цѣ - лит - - ся.
ra qu'il va gué - rir.
110
Fl.
p
Fl.
p
Cl.
Cl. bas.
m.d.
Fag.
T-ni
p
m.s.
Andante.
Клариче, мрачно, со злымъ предчувствіемъ.
111 Clarice, sombre, comme avec un mauvais pressentiment.
pp
Принцъ ис - цѣ - лит - ся, ког - да онъ за - смѣ - ет - ся...
Il va gué - rir quand on pour - ra le fai - re ri - re...
Леандръ
Léandre pp
Принцъ ис - цѣ - лит - ся, ког - да онъ за - смѣ - ет - ся...
Il va gué - rir quand on pour - ra le fai - re ri - re...
111 Andante.
pesante
p

Più mosso.
112 Энергично упрекая Леандра.
Reprochant énergiquement à Léandre.
Клар.
Clar.
А э-тотъ шутъ смѣшонъ.
Ce vil bouf-fon est drôle.
Вотъ ви-ди-те, къ че-
Vous êtes in-cor-ri-
Леан.
Léan.
Смѣшонъ.
C'est vrai.
112 Più mosso.
fz
Ob.
mf
m.s.
pp
T-be c. sord.
му ве-детъ ва-ша та-ка-я стран-на-я мед-ли-тельность.
gible, Léan-dre. Vo-tre lenteur de-vient e-xas-pé-ran-te.
mp
pp
mp
113
f
Прин-цу ну-женъ о-пій и-ли пу-ля.
Don-nez au Prince de l'o-pium ou une bal-le.
Quart. sul pontic.
Ob., Ob. c.-al.
f
ritard.
ritard. ff
Allegro.
114 Со стола падаетъ ваза. Леандръ и Клариче испуганно отступаютъ.
Un vase tombe de la table. Léandre et Clarice reculent terrifiés.
ff
Bassi, T-ni, Fag.
3
f

Леандръ
Léandre
115
Ударомъ ноги опрокидываетъ столъ. Подъ столомъ съежившаяся Смеральдина.
Léandre d'un coup de pied renverse la table, sous laquelle Sméraldine se trouve accroupie.
Что тамъ?
Qu'est_ce?
ff
116
Грозно.
Terrible.
Смеральдина встаетъ.
Sméraldine se lève.
Леан.
Léan.
Встань!
De_bout!
жал_ка_я змѣ -
fil _ le de ser -
T-ni
я!
pent!
Ты под_слу_ша_ла
Tu vou_lais surprendre
го_су _ дар_ствен_ну_ю
une af _ faire d'é_tat se -
C. F. e Fag.
117
118
Хочетъ крикнуть стражу.
Il veut appeler la garde.
тай_ну,
crè _ te.
и я те - бя каз - ню не_медленно!
Je vais de suite te fai - re pen - dre!
V-ni, Ob.
Quart., Fag., C. F.
T-ba c. sord.

Смеральдина, подбѣгаетъ къ Леандру и говоритъ серьезнымъ тономъ.
Sméraldine, accourt vers Léandre et lui parle d'un ton sérieux.
По-до-жди, Леандръ!
Un ins-tant, Léandre!
Не спѣ-ши съ каз-нью.
Lais-se moi vi-vre!
T-ba c. sord.
Смер.
Smér.
Те-бѣ гро-зитъ не-сча-стье:
Il faut que je te sau-ve:
pp V-ni con sord.
119
Тихо.
Tout bas.
За спи-но-ю
Der-rière le dos du
pp
Celli con sord.
Прин-ца сто-итъ
Prin-ce se tient

120
Смер.
Smér.
Труф - фаль - ди - но,
Trouf - fal - di - no,
а за спи - ной Труф - фаль - ди - но
et der - rière Trouf - fal - di - no
pp
сто - итъ Магъ Че - лій.
se tient le mage Tché - lio.
cresc.
mf
Poco più mosso.
121
Темнота. Въ глубинѣ сцены проходитъ освѣщенный Челій.
Obscurité. Au fond de la scène passe Tchélio éclairé.
Гля - ди.
Re - garde.
Леандръ
Léandre
Че - лій?
Tché - lio?
121 Poco più mosso.
pp misterioso
Bassi, C.F., G.Cassa

122
p T-ni con sord.
3
pp
pp
123
Cl.
p
Леандръ, подъ впечатлѣніемъ явленія.
Léandre, sous l'impression de l'apparition.
Poco più animato.
Какъ стран - - - - но!..
C'est é - tran - - - - ge!..
p
pizz.
Клариче, на которую появленіе Мага не произвело никакого впечатлѣнія.
Clarice, sur laquelle l'apparition de Tchélio n'a produit aucune impression.
И вотъ, Ле - андръ, что вы - - - - -
Et bien vo - yez, Lé - an - - - - -
p

124
Клар.
Clar.
шло: завтра празд-нества,
dre: de-main les fêtes com-mencent
cresc.
Драматично.
Dramatiquement.
125
и Принцъ смѣ-ет-ся!
et il va ri-re!
Cor.
f
Очень энергично.
Très énergiquement.
О-пій или пу-ля!
L'o-pium ou la bal-le!
pizz. e Fiati
m.s.
ff
G. P.
126
Указывая на Смеральдину.
Montrant Sméraldine.
А эту надо каз-
L'es-cla-ve, il faut la
pp Quart.
V-le
pp

127
Смеральдина
Sméraldine
Принцесса, Принцесса, есть спасенье отъ смѣха.
Princesse, Princesse, on pourra empêcher le rire.
Клар.
Clar.
нить.
tuer.
Celli e Fag.
espress.
128
Смер.
Smér.
Ob.
p
pp
Леандръ, съ тобою Фата Моргана.
Léandre, tu as pour toi Fata Morgana.
129
Она сама прійдетъ на праздне-
Elle va venir à cette fête elle mê-

130
Смер.
Smér.
ство, и Принцъ при ней
me. Près d'elle le Prince
cresc.
не за - смѣ - ет
ne peut pas ri
f
ся.
re.
ritard.
Andante assai.
Леандръ, потрясенный.
131 Léandre, émotionné.
Фа - та Мор - га - на?
Fa - ta Mor - ga - na?
espress.
Celli e Bassi con sord.
pp
Смеральдина
Sméraldine
132
Клариче, пораженная.
Clarice, saisie.
Да.
Oui.
Фа - та Мор - га - на?
Fa - ta Mor - ga - na?
Дѣлаютъ нѣсколько шаговъ впередъ и, протянувъ руки, призываютъ Фату Моргану.
Ils font quelques pas en avant et étendant les bras appellent Fata Morgana.
Леан.
Léan.
Ты отъ не - я?
Parles-tu pour elle?
Fl. e Celli
espress.
pp
Fag. e pizz.
132

Смер.
Smér.
Фа - та Мор - га - на!
Fa - ta Mor - ga - na!
Клар.
Clar.
Фа - та Мор - га - на!
Fa - ta Mor - ga - na!
Леан.
Léan.
Фа - та Мор - га - на!
Fa - ta Mor - ga - na!
V-ni, Fiati
cresc.
T-ni
pesante
Смер.
Smér.
Фа - та Мор - га - на!
Fa - ta Mor - ga - na!
Клар.
Clar.
Фа - та Мор - га - на!
Fa - ta Mor - ga - na!
Леан.
Léan.
Фа - та Мор - га - на!
Fa - ta Mor - ga - na!
T-be
Cor.
pp subito

133
Смер.
Smér.
p
Прій -
Ah,
Клар.
Clar.
p
Прій -
Ah,
Леан.
Léan.
p
Прій -
Ah,
cresc.
ff
133
ff
T-be
Cor.
Смер.
Smér.
f
ди къ намъ на празд - никъ!
viens pour la fê - te!
Клар.
Clar.
f
ди къ намъ на празд - никъ!
viens pour la fê - te!
Леан.
Léan.
f
ди къ намъ на празд - никъ!
viens pour la fê - te!
V-ni, Fiati
f
cresc.
ff
p subito
f
cresc.
ff

Смер.
Smér.
Сдѣ - лай намъ празд - никъ!
Fais pour nous une fê - te!
Клар.
Clar.
Сдѣ - лай намъ празд - никъ!
Fais pour nous une fê - te!
Леан.
Léan.
Сдѣ - лай намъ празд - никъ!
Fais pour nous une fê - te!
cresc.
p subito
cresc.
134
Фа - та Мор - га - на!
Fa - ta Mor - ga - na!
Фа - та Мор - га - на!
Fa - ta Mor - ga - na!
Фа - та Мор - га - на!
Fa - ta Mor - ga - na!
134
Занавѣсъ.
Rideau.
m.s.
p subito

АКТЪ II.

КАРТИНА I.

Спальня ипохондрическаго Принца. Принцъ сидитъ въ глубокомъ креслѣ, одѣтый въ карикатурную одежду больного. На головѣ компрессъ. Сбоку отъ него столъ, полный склянокъ, мазей, плевательницъ и другихъ приборовъ, соотвѣтствующихъ его состоянію.

ACTE II.

TABLEAU I.

La chambre du Prince hipocondriaque. Le Prince est assis dans un profond fauteuil, vêtu d'un costume (caricatural) de malade. Il a sur la tête une compresse, près de lui une table chargée de flacons, de pommades, de crachoirs et d'autres objets correspondant à son état.

138
Принцъ, больнымъ голосомъ.
Le Prince, d'une voix malade.
139
Ни - сколь - - - ко.
Ah, non, non...
Труффальдино, запыхавшись, но торжествуя.
Trouffaldino, haletant, mais d'un air victorieux.
Смѣш-но?
Est-ce drôle?
Не-у-
Est-ce pos-
139
Celli, Cor.
Пр.
Pr.
G.P.
Скуч - - но!
Non, non!
Вгла-
Ma
Труф.
Trouf.
же-ли не смѣш-но?
sible que je ne sois pas drôle?
Celli, Cor.
140
L'istesso tempo
захъ мель-ка-етъ, го-ло-ва бо-литъ, бо-ли въ пе-че-ни
vue se brouille, j'ai la tête en feu, des dou-leurs aux reins
Celli

141
Пр.
Pr.
и бо-ли въ поч - кахъ!
et des dou - leurs au foie!
Труффальдино, сочувственно.
Trouffaldino, compatissant.
Не
Tu
Ахъ, какъ не-пpi-ят-но!
Oh, comme c'est pé-ni-ble!
141
Moderato.
142
Стонетъ.
Gémissant.
ritard.
то-лько не-пpi-ят-но, но мно-го, мно-го ху-же... О! О!
dis que c'est pé-ni-ble. C'est pi-re, pi-re, pi-re!.. Oh! Oh!
Труф.
Trouf.
Что же
Qu'in-vente-
Cl.
Fag.
ritard.
142
Moderato.
Ob.
pizz.
О! О! О! О!
Oh! Oh! Oh! Oh!
дѣ-лать съ нимъ? Тан-цу-ешь — не смѣ-ет-ся, раз-ска-зы-ва-ешь — скуч-но, смѣ-
rais je en-core? Je dan-se — ça l'em-bê-te, je fais l'im-bé-cile — il ne rit

Принцъ закашлялся отъ своихъ стоновъ.
Les gémissements provoquent la toux.
143
Пр.
Pr.
O!
Oh!
Труф.
Trouf.
шшшь—онъ плачетъ. Я пря-мо вы-бил-ся изъ силъ! По-
pas, il pleu-re. Je suis au bout de mes res-sources! Je
V.I.
T-ni
Выдвинувши нижнюю челюсть, полную слюней, тычетъ рукой, требуя плевательницу.
Faisant ressortir la mâchoire pleine de salive il montre du doigt le crachoir qu'il exige.
144 Più mosso.
A
кашлять за-хо-тѣ-ли, Ва-ша Свѣтлость?
crois que votre Al-tes-se veut tous-ser?
pizz.
V-le sul pontic.
T-be con sord.
145
Плю-нуть за-хо-тѣ-ли, Ва-ша
Je crois que votre Al-tes-se veut cra-
pizz.

Тыча пальцемъ.
Indiquant nerveusement le crachoir du doigt.
poco
Плюетъ.
Crache.
146 Poco meno.
Пр.
Pr.
A!
A!
Тьфу.
Fft.
O
Oh
Подаетъ плевательницу.
Lui tend le crachoir.
Труффальдино принимаетъ плевательницу и изучаетъ ея содержимое; нюхаетъ.
Trouffaldino prend le crachoir, étudie son contenu, le renifle.
Труф.
Trouf.
Свѣт_лость?
cher?
Плюнь_те.
Fai_tes.
Fag.
T-ni
Quart. con sord.
Пах_нетъ ста_ры_ми, гни_лы_ми, и во_ню_чи_ми риѳ_ма_ми.
Ça sent des ri_mes pu_an_tes, j'ai de suite re_con_nu l'o_deur.
147 Più mosso.
Чудаки
Les Ridicules
Вотъ о_ни, мартелі_ан_скі_е сти_хи! Ка_на_лья!
Mais parbleu! Il le nourrit de vers mar_té_liens! Ca_nail_le!
Леандръ...
Léandre...
T-be c. sord.

rit. 148

Пр.
Pr.

Труффальдино
Trouffaldino

Принцъ, Ваша Свѣтлость, для васъ на-
Prince, votre Al_tes_se, on va don-

148

rit.

mfp

Труф.
Trouf.

зна_чи_ли та_кі_я празднества, что вы на_вѣр_но раз_смѣ_
ner de si bril_lan_tes fê_tes, que vous ri_rez, Prince, je vous

Fl.

p

149

Труф.
Trouf.

е_тесь. Да_вай_те о_дѣ_вать_ся и пой_
ju_re! Souf_frez qu'on vous ha_bil_le et par-

Fl., Ob.

f

f

pizz.

sf T-ni

Труф.
Trouf.

дем_те на нихъ.
tons sans re_tard.

f

mf

T-ni

Celli

Pochissimo meno.
150 Принцъ
Le Prince
О-дѣ-вать - - ся? Да
M'habil - ler, moi? C'est
Fl.,Cl.
lamentoso
mp
mf
p
Celli
V-ni e V-le
V-ni e V-le
151 Più animato.
Пр.
Pr.
ты со-шелъ съ у - ма!
fou ce qu'il me dit!
Труффальдино
Trouffaldino
Тамъ ве-се-ло, тамъ смѣхъ, тамъ
Cro - - yez, Al-tesse, c'est gai, on
151 Più animato.
p
mp
Fag.
152 Meno mosso.
Труф.
Trouf.
столь - ко раз-вле-че - - ній!
va nous fai-re ri - - re!
Комики, врываются на просценіумъ.
Les Comiques, se ruent sur le proscenium.
ff
Ко - ме - - дій! Ко-ме - - дій! Ве-
Don - nez nous du ri - - re, des
Meno mosso.
152
f Quart.

Ком. *Com.*

се - ла - го смѣ - ха! О - здо - ров - ля - ю - ща - го
vraies co - mé - di - es! Du rire jo - yeux, du rire so -

Чудаки
Les Ridicules

f Уй - ди - те!
Sor - tez d'i - ci,

pizz., Ob., Cor.

f

153

Ком. *Com.*

смѣ - ха! Бод - ря - щей ат - мо - сфе - ры!
no - re! Des scè - nes vi - vi - fian - tes!

Чуд. *Rid.*

Ско - рѣй уй - ди - те! Не мѣ -
sor - tez plus vi - te! Lais - sez

Ком. *Com.*

Яростно.
Avec fureur.

ff

Ко - ме - дій!
Du ri - re!

Чуд. *Rid.*

шай - те Труф - фаль - ди - но! Онъ дол - женъ спра - вить - ся безъ васъ! Уй -
fai - re Trouf - fal - di - no. Il peut, sans vous, gué - rir le Prince. Au

ff

p Quart.

f

154
Лопатами выгоняютъ Комиковъ, которые, отбиваясь, уходятъ за кулису.
Avec des pelles ils chassent les Comiques qui en se défendant sortent par la coulisse.
Чуд.
Rid.
ди - те!
dia_ble!
Quart.
154
T-be, T-ni
f tempestoso
cresc.
8
ff Tutti
155
mp Quart.
T-be
f
T-ni
T-ni
Quart.
f
ben tenuto

156
Чудаки, утомленные, возвращаются въ башни.
Les Ridicules, fatigués, rentrent dans les tours.
f
mp
p un poco calando
Принцъ
Le Prince
p
rit.
О...
Oh...
157
Tempo di Marcia animata.
Труффальдино
Trouffaldino
p
Слушайте...
At_ten_tion...
3 T-be e 2
T-ni con sord.,
Piatti, Triang.,
T.mil., Arpa.
За кулисами музыка веселаго марша.
On entend de la coulisse la musique d'une marche gaie.
pp
pp
Bassi
rit.
Труф.
Trouf.
Слушайте...
que c'est beau!..
Тамъ уже началось...
On com_men_ce...
Скорѣй идемте!
Allons plus vi_te!
p
f

Принцъ
Le Prince
158
Перебивая.
L'interrompant.
Не пой - ду.
Non, je reste.
Дай мнѣ э - то - го ле - кар - - - ства!
Don - ne moi de cette méde - ci - - - ne!
Труф.
Trouf.
Ахъ, до че - го...
Oh, à quel point...
Ахъ, до че-
Oh, à quel
pp
158
го тамъ будетъ ве - се - ло!
point c'est a - mu - sant là - bas!
Вотъ ва - ша ман - ті - я.
Met - tez ce grand man - teau,
На - дѣнь - те е - е по - верхъ бѣ - лья.
met - tez le sim - ple - ment sur la che - mise.
pp
159
Принцъ, кричитъ капризно.
Le Prince, crie capricieusement.
ff
Дай мнѣ э - тихъ
Don - ne moi ces
tacet
159
Quart.
f

Пр.
Pr.
ка - - - - - - - - - - - - - - - пель!
gout - - - - - - - - - - - - - - - tes!
Труф.
Trouf.
Разгорячившись.
S'échauffant.
Капли не по -
Ce n'est pas la
m.s.
Кап - - - - - ли!
Vi - - - - - te,
мо - гутъ!
pei - ne!
Двад - - - - - цать
quin - - - - - ze
V.I.
160
ка - - пель!
gout - - - tes!
Разсердившись, какъ на капризнаго ребенка.
Se fâchant comme avec un enfant capricieux.
Каплямъ мѣсто за о - кош - комъ!
Voi - là où vont par - tir les gout - tes!
Des
Ob. e V. I.
T-be con sord.

161
Пр.
Pr.
Кап - - - - - - - - ли!!
gout - - - - - - - - - tes!!
Труф.
Trouf.
Выбрасывая склянки.
Jetant les flacons.
Въ ок-но! Въ ок-
Voi-là, par-
Выбрасываетъ въ окно всѣ склянки и плевательницы.
Il jette par la fenêtre tous les flacons et crachoirs.
Tutti
161
Съ плачемъ.
Pleurant.
Какъ ты смѣ - ешь? Без - бож - никъ! Раз -
Quelle au - da - ce! Ca - nail - le! In -
но! Въ ок-но!
tez, par-tez!
Въ ок - но!
En - core!
бой - никъ! Ка - на - лья!
fâ - me! Fri - pouil - le!
Въ ок - но!
Voi - là!
Те - перь и -
Et puis, en

162

Пр.
Pr.

Ахъ! Ахъ! Ахъ!
Ah! Ah! Ah!

Накрывъ мантiей, взваливаетъ его на плечи.
En le couvrant avec le manteau, il le saisit et l'emporte sur son épaule.

Труф.
Trouf.

дем - те!
rou - te!

162

f

f 3 Cor., Celli

163

Принцъ, теряя компрессъ, отбиваясь и плача.
Le Prince, *se défendant, pleurant et perdant sa compresse.*

f

От - пу - сти! От - пу -
Lâ - che moi! Lâ - che

Cl., V-le

Пр.
Pr.

сти! Я у - мру! Я у -
moi! J'en mour - rai! J'en mour-

Fl., V.II. 8

8 *f*

Труффальдино уноситъ его.
Trouffaldino l'emporte.
164
Принцъ кричитъ благимъ матомъ.
Le Prince crie à tue tête.
Пр.
Pr.
мру!
rai!
A!
Ah!
A!
Ah!
ff
ff
165
Занавѣсъ.
Rideau.
Quart.
Quart.
T-ne,
Tuba
fp
cresc.
T-be
f
166
ff
ff
Tutti

167
T-be
mf
V-ni.T-ba.Fl.
V-ni,Fiati
168
T-be
T-ba,V.I,Fl.,Ob.
169
ff Tutti
Quart.
mf

170
T-be,Cor.
V.I,Cl.
p
171
V-ni,Ob.
T-be,Cor.
Cor.
T-ba c.sord.
T-be, Cor.
V.I, Fl.
V-ni,Fiati
V.I,Fl.,Picc.
T-ba c. sord.
cresc.
T-be,Cor.
ff
172
Tutti

КАРТИНА II.

TABLEAU II.

Большой дворъ королевскаго дворца. На крытой терассѣ Король, Клариче и Принцъ, укутанный въ мантію и шубы. На другихъ терассахъ придворные дамы и кавалеры, также Леандръ и Панталонъ.

La grande cour du palais royal. Sur une véranda le Roi, Clarice et le Prince enveloppé dans un manteau et des fourrures. Sur des terraces des dames et des courtisans, ainsi que Léandre et Pantalon.

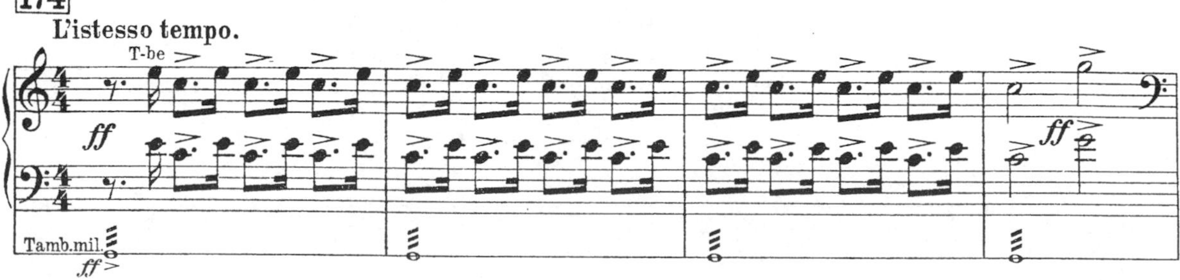

Появляются уроды съ огромными головами.
Apparaissent des monstres avec des têtes immenses.
176
Cor.
f molto pesante
f
cresc.
ff
177
Труффальдино, командуетъ уродамъ.
Trouffaldino, ordonne aux monstres.
Впередъ! Впередъ!
Al_lez! Al_lez!
Придворные
Les courtisans
f
Бра - во, бра - во, бра - во!
Bien! Bra - vo, bra - vo!
177
Quart.
T-ni
3

Происходитъ бой уродовъ на дубинахъ. Труффальдино указываетъ имъ смѣшныя движенія.
Une bataille avec des massues a lieu entre les monstres. Trouffaldino leur indique des mouvements grotesques.
178
Труф.
Trouf.
Впе_редъ!
Hol_là!
T-ni, Timp., Bassi, Fag.
V. I, Ob., Ob. c-al.
V. II, V-le, Cl.
T-be
179
Cor.
T-be, Cor.
V. I, Ob.
V. II, V-le, Cl.

180
T-be
T-ni
181
brioso
Одна группа уродовъ побѣждаетъ другую.
Un groupe de monstres est victorieux.
ritard.
Animato.
182
Придворные, апплодируя.
Les courtisans, applaudissant.
Бра - во, бра - во, бра - во! О - чень ин - те - рес - но!
Bien! Bra - vo, bra - vo! C'est in - com - pa - ra - ble!
Animato.
182
Quart.

Труффальдино, поднимаясь на ступени королевской терассы.
Trouffaldino, montant sur les marches de la véranda royale.
Смѣ - ял - ся ли Принцъ?
Le Prince, a - t-il ri?
Придв.
Court.
pp
За - мѣ - ча - тель - но ве - се - ло!
C'est très gai, c'est vrai - ment par - fait!
Бра - во, бра - во, бра - во, бра - во!
Oh, bra - vo, bra - vo, bra - vo!
f
Cl., Fag. e pizz.
Poco meno mosso.
Принцъ, плачущимъ голосомъ.
Le Prince, d'une voix pleurnicharde.
183
ad libitum
p
f
Король
Le Roi
Шумъ о - глу - ша - етъ мнѣ го - ло - ву!
Ce bruit me fa - ti - gue la tê - te!
Воз - духъ без - по -
L'air est né -
Нѣтъ.
Non.
183
Poco meno mosso.
V-le tr
fp
T-ni
colla parte
Cl.
pp
Cl. bas.
Пр.
Pr.
ко - итъ мнѣ лег - кі - я!
faste à mon pau - vre cœur!
Король.
Roi.
Даль - ше!
Ah! c'est mal!
Труффальдино, уродамъ.
Trouffaldino, aux monstres.
184
Ступай - те вонъ!
Al - lez vous en!
Мечется по сценѣ, приготовляя слѣдующій дивертисментъ.
Il court très agité sur la scène préparant le divertissement suivant.
V-le tr
Cl.
pp
Cl. bas.
Celli e Bassi
f energico
184
T-be, T-ni, Quart.
V-le
f

Фата Моргана появляется на авансценѣ, одѣтая ветхой старушонкой.
Fata Morgana apparait sur l'avant-scène habillée en vieille femme.
Леандръ, увидѣвъ такое неподобающее для королевскаго двора явленіе, подходитъ къ ней.
Léandre, remarquant une apparition si étrange à la cour royale, s'approche de Fata Morgana.
V-ni
T-be con sord.
mf
f espress.
Celli, Bassi
V-le
Леандръ
Léandre
Кто ты? Что тебѣ на_до?
Qui es tu? Qu'est ce que tu cher_ches?
V-ni
mp espress.
Cor. e Celli
Фата Моргана
Fata Morgana
185
Я Фа_та Мор_
Je suis Fa_ta Mor_
pp misterioso
Проходитъ въ кулису.
Elle sort dans la coulisse.
Фата.
Fata.
га_на. По_ка я здѣсь, Принцъ не за_смѣ_ет_ся.
ga_na. Quand je suis là, il ne peut pas ri_re.
pp

Леандръ, молитвенно складывая руки ей во слѣдъ.
Léandre, la suit des yeux joignant dévotement les mains.
186
Бла-го-дѣ-тель-ни-ца! Ца-ри-ца и-по-
Bien-fai-tri-ce! Oh, reine d'hypocon-
mf
Celli Ob. c.ra.
con Ped.
V-ni, Cl.
fp
f
Cor.
Fag.
Леан.
Léan.
хон-дрі-и!..
dri-e!..
V-ni, Fl, Cl.
Animato.
ff
Tamb. mil.
187
Труффальдино, объявляетъ съ большимъ подъемомъ.
Trouffaldino, déclarant avec entrain.
Ди-вер-тис-ментъ но-меръ вто-рой! От-
Di-ver-tisse-ment nu-mé-ro deux! Ou-
Quart. e Fag.
p
Труф.
Trouf.
крыть фонта-ны!
vrez les fon-tai-nes!
188
Открываютъ первый фонтанъ.
On ouvre la première fontaine.
Торжественно докладываетъ.
Il déclare pompeusement.
Бьетъ масломъ.
C'est de l'hui-le.
gliss.
Arpa
pp
Picc.
T-ni Cor.

189
Труф.
Trouf.
Бьетъ ви-номъ!
C'est du vin!
Придворные
Les courtisans
Апплодируя.
En applaudissant.
О!
Oh!
Бра - во!
Bien! bien!
V-ni
Открываютъ второй фонтанъ.
On ouvre la deuxième fontaine.
Arpa gliss.
m.d.
C.F.
Стражѣ.
Aux gardes.
poco rit.
Пу-скай-те пьяницъ и об-жоръ!
A-me-nez les iv-rognes et les gloutons!
Очень ин-те-рес-но!
Oh, c'est ad-mi-ra-ble!
Ис-клю-чи-тель-но тон-ко!
C'est d'un goût re-mar-ca-ble!
Придв.
Court.
T-be, T-ni

Стража отворяетъ ворота. Пьяницы и обжоры съ ведрами и всякаго рода посудою, толкаясь и торопясь, устремляются къ фонтанамъ.

Les gardes ouvrent les grandes portes. Les ivrognes et gloutons aves des seaux et d'autres récipients se précipitent en se bousculant vers les fontaines.

193
Самъ хохочетъ, наслаждаясь
ихъ давкою и ссорами.
Il rit se réjouissant de la
bousculade et de la querelle.
Cor.
V-ni
Fiati
3 T-be
T-ni
Tutti
194
Труффальдино, поднимаясь на ступени королевской терассы.
Trouffaldino, montant les marches de la véranda royale.
Смѣ - ял - ся ли
Le Prince, a - t - il
V-le
Fag.
Celli pizz.
Труф.
Trouf.
Принцъ?
ri?
Король
Le Roi
Нѣтъ.
Non.
195
Принцъ, плача.
Le Prince, pleurant.
Ой, от - не - си - те ме - ня въ теп - лу - ю по -
Oh, met - tez moi, met - tez moi dans un lit bien douil -
rit.
T-ni, Tuba, Piatti
Bassi
Cl.

196
Пр.
Pr.
стель!
let!
Труффальдино
Trouffaldino
Ахъ, ка-ко-е го-ре!
Je n'ai pas de chan-ce!
Стра-жа! Го-
Gar-des! Chas-
Король
Le Roi
Даль-ше.
Ah! c'est mal.
196
Celli, Bas., Fag.
Cor.
Quart.
L'istesso tempo.
Стража тѣснитъ пьяницъ и обжоръ обратно въ ворота.
Les gardes repoussent vers les portes les ivrognes et les gloutons.
197
marcatissimo
Труф.
Trouf.
ни-те ихъ вонъ! Что имъ тутъ тол-кать-ся!
sez tout ce monde! Qu'ont ils à se bat-tre!
Ob. c-a.
Труффальдино, разстроенный, выходитъ на авансцену.
Trouffaldino, contrarié, s'avance sur le devant de la scène.
Труф.
Trouf.
Ну, что я мо-гу сдѣ-
Que puis je en-core faire pour

198
poco rit.
Poco meno mosso.
Труф.
Trouf.
лать? Онъ хо - четъ въ теплу - ю по-стель!
lui? Il veut a - voir un lit douil-let!
pizz.
Quart., Arpe
V-ni, Fl., Picc.
Фата Моргана ковыляетъ изъ кулисы.
Fata Morgana arrive en titubant par la coulisse.
199
mp espress.
Celli
200 Vivace.
Фата Моргана
Fata Morgana
А тебѣ ка-ко - е дѣ-ло? А
Ça ne te re-gar - de pas. Quel
Труффальдино, разстроенный неудачами, накидывается на Фату Моргану.
Trouffaldino, contrarié par son échec s'en prend à Fata Morgana.
Ты кто та-ка-я?! Какъ ты смѣешь здѣсь ходить?
Qui est cette femme?! Qui l'a fait en-trer i-ci?
200 Vivace.
col legno e Fiati
pizz. e Fiati
201
Фата.
Fata.
ты какъ смѣешь при-ста - вать? От - стань!
droit as tu de com-man - der? Laisse moi!
Труф.
Trouf.
Здѣсь те - бѣ не мѣ - сто. Сту -
Ce n'est pas ta pla - ce. Va
Quart., Fag., Timp.

Фата.
Fata.
Труф.
Trouf.
Про-па-ди!
Qu'as tu dit?
пай сей-часъ же!
t'en de sui-te!
Та-ка-я грязь, какъ ты, и смѣ-ешь
Une telle sale-té comme toi, tu o-ses
202
a tempo
Ахъ, не-год-ный! Не-год-ный, не-год-ный!
Ah, quelle bru-te! Quelle bru-te, quelle bru-te!
poco rit.
здѣсь ходить!
être i-ci?
За во-ро-та, за во-ро-та! Ско-
A la por-te, à la por-te! Va
V-ni
colla parte
Fag.
Падаетъ, высоко задравши ноги.
Elle tombe en relevant très haut les jambes.
Пусти, пусти! Не тро-гай! Ah!!
As-sez, as-sez! Lâche moi! Ah!!
Толкаетъ ее.
Il la pousse.
рѣй! Ну, ско-рѣй же! У-би-рай-ся вонъ! Ахъ, про-
t'en, vas plus vi-te! Fi-che moi la paix! Ah, mau-
T-be

203
Più mosso. Molto animato.
Труф.
Trouf.
кля - та - я!
di - te!
V-ni, Cl.
Принцъ, поднимается изъ кресла.
Le Prince, se soulevant du fauteuil.
Ха - ха...
Ha - ha...
ха - ха - ха...
ha - ha - ha...
V. I
204
Пр.
Pr.
ха - ха - ха - ха...
ha - ha - ha - ha...
ха -
ha -
V. II
ха - ха - ха - ха...
ha - ha - ha - ha...
ха - ха...
ha - ha...
V-le

205
Смѣхъ становится все громче и радостнѣе.
Le rire devient de plus en plus fort et joyeux.
Пр.
Pr.
ха, ха - ха, ха - ха, ха - ха, ха - ха, ха - ха, ха -
ha, ha - ha, ha - ha, ha - ha, ha - ha, ha - ha, ha -
etc.
p
ха, ха! Ха - ха, ха - ха, ха - ха, ха - ха, ха -
ha, ha! Ha - ha, ha - ha, ha - ha, ha - ha, ha -
206
ха, ха - ха, ха - ха, ха! Ха - ха, ха -
ha, ha - ha, ha - ha, ha! Ha - ha, ha -
Quart.
Fl.
ac - ce - le -
ха, ха - ха, ха - ха, ха - ха - ха - ха, ха -
ha, ha - ha, ha - ha, ha - ha - ha - ha, ha -
mp

ran - - - do
207 Più mosso.
Пр.
Pr.
ха - ха - ха - ха!
ha - ha - ha - ha!
Ха - ха - ха, ха - ха - ха, ха - ха - ха, ха - ха - ха, ха - ха - ха,
Ha - ha - ha, ha - ha - ha, ha - ha - ha, ha - ha - ha, ha - ha - ha,
f p
pizz.
208
più accelerando
ха - ха - ха, ха - ха - ха, ха - ха - ха - ха!
ha - ha - ha, ha - ha - ha, ha - ha - ha - ha!
Ха - ха - ха - ха, ха - ха - ха - ха,
Ha - ha - ha - ha, ha - ha - ha - ha,
Cl., Fag.
mp
209
Захлебываясь.
Suffoquant de rire.
poco a poco
ха - ха - ха - ха, ха - ха - ха - ха!
ha - ha - ha - ha, ha - ha - ha - ha!
Ка - ка - я...
Cette vieil - le...
f
pizz.
mf
ri - - - - - tar - - - - - dan - - -
смѣш - на - я... ста - ру - шон -
cette vieil - le... est si drô -
mp

210 Meno mosso.
Пр.
Pr.
do
ка!
le!
Fl.
14
15
16
p
pizz.
V. I
V. II
Cl.bas.
pp
pizz.
Король
Le Roi
211 Allegro non troppo.
mf
За-смѣ-ял-ся!..
Ah, le ri-re!..
f
За-смѣ
Oui, le
Придворные
Les courtisans
Полушопотомъ.
p A demi-voix.
За-смѣ-ял-ся...
C'est le ri-re...
Чудаки
Les Ridicvles
211 Allegro non troppo.
Quart.
p T-be, T-ni
cresc.

Труффальдино
Trouffaldino
ff
За-смѣ - ял - ся Принцъ!
Il a ri, le Prince!
Панталонъ
Pantalon
ff
За-смѣ - ял - ся Принцъ!
Il a ri, le Prince!
Король.
Roi.
ff
За-смѣ - ял - ся Принцъ!
Il a ri, le Prince!
Придв.
Court.
ff
ял - ся! За-смѣ - ял - ся Принцъ!
ri - re! Il a ri, le Prince!
Чуд.
Rid.
ff
За-смѣ - ял - ся Принцъ!
Il a ri, le Prince!
ff Tutti

212
Труф.
Trouf.
ff
Ха, ха-ха-ха, ха-ха - ха, ха-ха-ха, ха-ха-
Ha, ha-ha-ha, ha-ha - ha, ha-ha-ha, ha-ha-
Пант.
Pant.
Ха, ха-ха-ха, ха-ха - ха, ха-ха-ха, ха-ха-
Ha, ha-ha-ha, ha-ha - ha, ha-ha-ha, ha-ha-
Король.
Roi.
Ха, ха-ха-ха, ха-ха - ха, ха-ха-ха, ха-ха-
Ha, ha-ha-ha, ha-ha - ha, ha-ha-ha, ha-ha-
Придв.
Court.
Ха, ха-ха-ха, ха-ха - ха, ха-ха-ха, ха-ха-
Ha, ha-ha-ha, ha-ha - ha, ha-ha-ha, ha-ha-
Чуд.
Rid.
Ха, ха-ха-ха, ха-ха - ха, ха-ха-ха, ха-ха-
Ha, ha-ha-ha, ha-ha - ha, ha-ha-ha, ha-ha-
212
fff

213
Труф.
Trouf.
ха, ха-ха-ха, ха-ха - ха, ха-ха-ха, ха-ха - ха!
ha, ha-ha-ha, ha-ha - ha, ha-ha-ha, ha-ha - ha!
Пант.
Pant.
ха, ха-ха-ха, ха-ха - ха, ха-ха-ха, ха-ха - ха!
ha, ha-ha-ha, ha-ha - ha, ha-ha-ha, ha-ha - ha!
Король.
Roi.
ха, ха-ха-ха, ха-ха - ха, ха-ха-ха, ха-ха - ха!
ha, ha-ha-ha, ha-ha - ha, ha-ha-ha, ha-ha - ha!
Придв.
Court.
ха, ха-ха-ха, ха-ха - ха, ха-ха-ха, ха-ха - ха!
ha, ha-ha-ha, ha-ha - ha, ha-ha-ha, ha-ha - ha!
Чуд.
Rid.
ха, ха-ха-ха, ха-ха - ха, ха-ха-ха, ха-ха - ха!
ha, ha-ha-ha, ha-ha - ha, ha-ha-ha, ha-ha - ha!
213
T-be e T-ni
ff

Отъ избытка радости всѣ порывисто пляшутъ. Со всего двора пало тяжелое бремя. Король приплясываетъ, сидя на своемъ тронѣ. Только Клариче и Леандръ не раздѣляютъ веселья.

Par excès de joie tout le monde danse d'une façon saccadée. La cour est libérée d'un grand poids. Le Roi esquisse une danse restant assis sur son trône. Seuls Clarice et Léandre ne partagent pas la joie générale.

Andante assai.
Пляска вдругъ прекращается. Фата Моргана грозно и медленно поднимается. Свѣтъ темнѣетъ. Придворные въ ужасѣ пятятся къ выходу.
216
La danse s'arrête soudainement. Fata Morgana se lève lentement d'une façon terrifiante. La lumière pâlit. Les courtisans, terrifiés, reculent vers la sortie.
T-ni con sord.
Quart.
espress.
Tam-tam
m.s.
m.d.
Фата Моргана, яростно, Принцу.
217
Fata Morgana, férocement au Prince.
Вар - варъ! Слу - шай! Слу - шай мо - е за -
Mon - stre! E - cou - te! E - cou - te mon a - na -
Quart.
C. F. e
G. Cass.
Фата.
Fata.
кля - тье! Вар - варъ! Слу - - - - -
thè - me! Mon - stre! E - - - - -

218
Изъ всѣхъ щелей, изъ подъ ступеней терассъ, появляются чертенята, которые окружаютъ Фату Моргану.
De toutes parts, de dessous les marches de la véranda apparaissent des petits diables qui entourent Fata Morgana.
Фата.
Fata.
шай!
coute!
V-ni
f
mf
cresc.
Fag. e pizz.
Заклинаетъ.
Prononce une malédiction.
219
Чертенята, воютъ.
Les petits diables, hurlent.
mf legato
Влю -
Il
И!
Hi!
V-ni
ff
бись
faut
въ три
que
а
tu
пель
su
Черт.
Diab.

Фата.
Fata.
си - - - - - - - - - на! Влю -
bis - - - - - - - - - ses l'a -
Черт.
Diab.
И!
Hi!
5
m.d.
3
T-be,
T-ni,
Timp,
Piatti
ff
3
Фата.
Fata.
бись въ три а - - - - - пель - - - -
mour pour trois o - - - -
Черт.
Diab.
И!
Hi!

Фата.
Fata.
си - - - - - - - - - - на! Влю -
ran - - - - - - - - - ges, l'a -
И!
Hi!
Черт.
Diab.
m. d.
T-be,
T-ni,
Timp.,
Piatti
ff
Фата.
Fata.
бись въ три а - - - пель - - - -
mour pour trois o - - - -
И!
Hi!
Черт.
Diab.

Фата.
Fata.
си
ran
Черт.
Diab.
И!
Hi!
на!
ges!
T-be, T-ni, Cor., Timp.
m. s.
veloce
220

Фата.
Fata.
Сквозь у-гро-зы, сквозь мольбы и сле-зы, день и ночь,— бѣ-
A travers les plain-tes et me-na-ces, jour et nuit,— tu
Черт.
Diab.
Воютъ.
Hurlent.
И!
Hi!
Quart., Cor. con sord.
mp espress.
221
ги,— бѣ-ги,— бѣ-
mar-ches, tu cher-ches, tu
Quart.
C. F. e
G. Cass.

Фата.
Fata.
ги къ тремъ а пель - си - намъ! Бѣ -
cherches les trois o - ran - ges! Dé -
fp
Черт.
Diab.
И!
Hi!
ги! Бѣ ги!!
si - re! Dé - si - re!!
ff
Фата Моргана исчезаетъ вмѣстѣ съ чертенятами. Придворные и стража разбѣгаются. Остаются только Король, Принцъ, Панталонъ и Труффальдино.
Fata Morgana disparaît avec les diables. Les courtisans et la garde fuient. Il ne reste que le Roi, le Prince, Pantalon et Trouffaldino.
222
T-ni c. sord. e Timp.
6 Cor.
Tuba, Tam-tam

Сцена понемногу свѣтлѣетъ.
La scène petit-à-petit redevient claire.
223 L'istesso tempo.
Poco più mosso.
Чудаки
Les Ridicules
Ахъ, какое горе!
Ah, quelle catastrophe!
V-le
Fag.
Ob. c.-a.
dim.
Принцъ
Le Prince
224 Allegro non troppo.
Начинаетъ приходить въ неописуемое волненіе.
Commence à éprouver une agitation indescriptible.
Три апельсина...
Les trois oranges...
V-le.
Celli
Пр.
Pr.
три апельсина...
les trois oranges...
Bassi pizz.
V-ni
Bassi
Fiati

225 Стремглавъ бросается на просценiумъ. Панталонъ и Труффальдино пытаются его поймать.
Le Prince se rue sur le proscenium. Pantalon et Trouffaldino tâchent de l'attraper.
Пр.
Pr.
Три а-пельси-на! Три а-пельси-на! Три а-пель-си-на!
Ah, trois o-ran-ges! Ah, trois o-ran-ges! Ah, trois o-ran-ges!
V. I e Fl.
f
p
8
p
Пр.
Pr.
Три а-пель-си-на!
Ah, trois o-ran-ges!
8
mf
T-be
226 Труффальдино, ловя Принца.
Trouffaldino, tâchant d'attraper le Prince.
Ахъ! Ахъ... ахъ...
Ah! Ah... ah...
Панталонъ, ловя Принца.
Pantalon, tâchant d'attraper le Prince.
Принцъ! Принцъ... Ахъ, что слу-
Prince! Prince... Ah, quelle his-
226
mp

Труф.
Trouf.
Принцъ!
Prince!
Пант.
Pant.
чи- - -лось!
toi- - -re!
Ахъ!
Ah!
Fl., Cl., Arpe
mp leggiero
Принцъ, пойманный, старается вырваться.
Le Prince, étant attrapé, essaye de s'échapper.
227
ff
rit.
a tempo
Три а-пель-си-на!
Trois o-ran-ges!
Пант.
Pant.
Ахъ!
Ah!
227
colla parte
a tempo
f pizz.
T-ni
p
Пр.
Pr.
О-ни у Кре-он- - - - - -ты, я зна-ю!
Elles sont chez Cré-on- - - - - -te, sans dou-te!
V. I
Fl., Picc.
pp scherzando
V. I
p

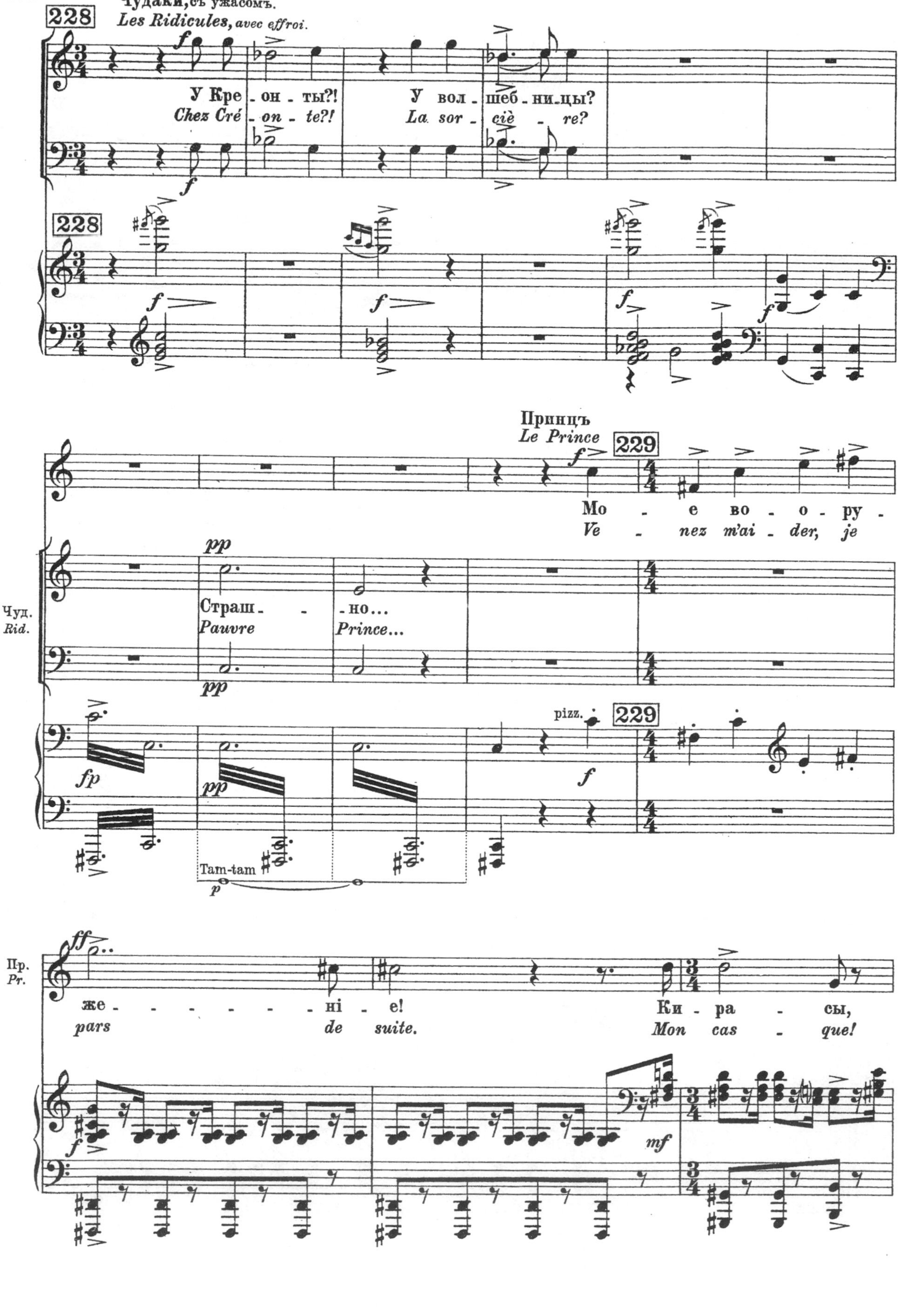

228

Чудаки, съ ужасомъ.
Les Ridicules, avec effroi.

У Кре - оны?! У вол - шеб - ни - цы?
Chez Cré - on - te?! La sor - ciè - re?

228

Принцъ
Le Prince

229

Мо - е во - о - ру -
Ve - nez m'ai - der, je

Чуд.
Rid.

Страш - но...
Pauvre Prince...

pizz.

229

Tam-tam

230
Энергично.
Energiquement.
Пр.
Pr.
шле - мы, ме - чи!
Vi - - te, l'é - pée!
Труф-фаль-
Trouf-fal-
Панталонъ Pantalon
Принцъ... Принцъ... ахъ!
Prince... Prince... ah!
f
fp
Ob.c-a, Fag.
ди - но, ты от - пра-вишься со мной.
di - no, je t'em - mè - ne a - vec moi.
Ско-рѣй! Ско-
Plus vite! Plus
Труффальдино
Trouffaldino
Страш - но... ой, какъ страш - но!
Pauvre moi... Ça me trou - ble!
Ob.
mf
p
231
рѣй!
vite!
Король, приближаясь къ Принцу.
Le Roi, s'approchant du Prince.
Ку - да ты,
De grâ - ce,
Fag., V-le, Celli
subito f
T-ni

Горячо.
Chaleureusement.
232
Пр.
Pr.
И - скать три а-пель-си - на, мо-е сча-стье, мо-ю лю-бовь!
Je veux les trois o - ran - ges, mon bon - heur et mon seul a - mour!
Король
Roi
сынъ мой?
Prin - ce!
232
Quart.
espress.
pp
mf
233
Пр.
Pr.
Король
Roi
О - ста - но - вись,
Ar - rê - te toi,
233
Fag., V-le, Celli
f
p
T-ni
234
Пр.
Pr.
О - ни то - мят - ся у Кре - он - ты, у Кре-
Elles sont cap - ti - ves chez Cré - on - te, chez Cré-
Король
Roi
сынъ мой...
Prin - - - ce...
234
Quart. espress.
pp
p
mf

235
Пр.
Pr.
он - ты... Я дол - женъ взять ихъ!
on - te... Je dois les pren - dre!
Король
Roi
По - ду - май,
Ton sort m'an -
235
mf
f Quart.
f
p
T-ni
Король
Roi
сынъ мой! Те - бѣ быть мо-жетъ гро - зитъ у
gois - - - - se. Mon fils, tu cours des dan - gers. Je
Cor.
T-ne
pp
236
Труффальдино, трагично.
Trouffaldino, tragiquement.
p
И смерть...
La mort...
Панталонъ, трагично.
Pantalon, tragiquement.
И
La
Король
Roi
жас-на-я ги - - - бель— и смерть!
vois des pé - rils et la mort!
236
pp
p mf Fag.
dim.

237

Принцъ, восторженно.
Le Prince, exalté.

Люб - лю, люб - лю, люб -
J'a - dore, j'a - dore, j'a -

лю три а - пель - си - - на! Ско - рѣ - е!
dore trois o - ran - - ges! Plus vi - te!

Ско - рѣ - е!
Plus vi - te!

Пант.
Pant.

смерть...
mort...

Король, болѣе твердымъ голосомъ.
Le Roi, d'une voix plus ferme.

Я не пу - щу те - бя:
Non, je m'op - po - se.

Король
Roi

ты мой на - слѣд - никъ, и дол - женъ ду - мать
Pense au ro - yau - me. Toi, l'hé - ri - tier, tu en

V. I

V-ni

Fl. Picc.

pp scherzando

Fag.

Ob. V-ni

f p

mf p.

238

Пр.
Pr.

Пр.
Pr.
Король
Roi
Люб - - лю, люб -
J'a - - dore, j'a -
о го - су - дар - ствѣ.
es res - pon - sa - ble.
V.I
Fl. Picc.
pp scherzando
лю! Не на - до го-су-дар - ства!
dore! Au dia - ble le ro-yau - me!
239
Ты не пой -
C'est im-pos -
Fiati
cresc.
Celli e Bassi
Нѣтъ, ни за что!
Pour rien au monde!
дешь. По-ве-лѣ-ва - ю те-бѣ о - стать - ся. При -
sible. Tu dois res - ter lors-que je l'e - xi - ge. C'est
V-ni
Fiati
V.I

Машетъ руками.
Agitant les bras.
Пр.
Pr.
Нѣтъ!
Non!
Нѣтъ!
Non!
Король
Roi
ка - зы - ва - ю!
moi qui or - donne!
Fiati
V-ni
cresc.
240 Meno mosso.
Пораженный.
Bouleversé.
Ты под - ни - ма - ешь ру - ку на от -
Quoi, tu as pu le - ver la main sur
Cello solo, molto vibrato
Cl.
Принцъ облачается въ кирасы.
Le Prince met sa cuirasse.
Ско - рѣ - е, Труффальди - но!
Plus vi - te, Trouffal - di - no!
Скорбно.
Tristement.
ца?..
moi?..
Сынъ на от - ца...
Un fils contre un père...
сынъ на от -
un fils contre un

Панталонъ, патетически.
Pantalon, pathétique.
241
Вуль-
Ces
Король
Roi
mf
ff
ца! От - ку-да э-то? На-вѣр-но-е изъ пошлыхъ фар-совъ!
père! A qui la fau-te? La faute est à ces sa-les far-ces!
Cello
p
241
p pizz.
p
f
Пант.
Pant.
242
Врываются Пустоголовые.
Les Têtes Vides font irruption.
гар - ныхъ фар-совъ!
farces vul - gai-res!
Fiati
p
Cor.
Allegro.
f veloce
Пустоголовые
Têtes Vides
f
243
Фар-совъ! Фар-совъ! За-нят-ной е-рун-ды! Дву-
Vi-te, vi-te, des far-ces a-mu-santes, des
f
f
ff mp

Король, топаетъ ногой и нервно кричитъ на нихъ.
Le Roi, excité, frappe du pied et crie contre les Têtes Vides.
Вонъ! Сей - часъ же
Sor - tez de sui - te!
Пусто-голов.
Têtes Vides
смысл - ен - ныхъ ост - ротъ! На - ряд - ныхъ туа -
mots d'es - prit gri - vois! Don - nez nous du
244
Король
Roi
у - хо - ди - те!
A la por - te!
ле - товъ!
lu - xe!
Хо - тимъ не ду - мать и смѣ - ять - ся!
Ne pas pen - ser, mais ri - re, ri - re!
Чудаки, выскакивая изъ башенъ.
Les Ridicules, sautant des tours.
Сту - пай - те! Сту -
Si - len - ce! Si -
f
mf

Meno mosso.
A tempo
245
Выгоняютъ ихъ лопатами.
Les chassent avec leurs pelles.
Чуд.
Rid.
пай - те! И
len - ce! C'est
такъ здѣсь тя - же - ло.
bien as - sez pé - nible!
Cor. e Quart.
T-ni, Timp.
Пустоголовые, отступая.
Têtes Vides, reculant.
Фар_совъ!
Far_ces!
Tutti
Чудаки, прогнавъ Пустоголовыхъ, возвращаются въ башни.
Les Ridicules, ayant chassé les Têtes Vides, rentrent dans leurs tours.
246
T-ni
f pesante
Принцъ, готовый въ путь.
Le Prince, prêt pour le voyage.
Про -
A -
T-ne
p ritard.

247 Un poco maestoso.
Пр.
Pr.
щай, о тецъ.
dieu, mon père.
p Cor.
p
248
Пр.
Pr.
Вѣдь ес_либъ я о_стал_ся, я сно_ва впалъ бы въ ме_лан_хо_лі_ю...
Je crois que si je res_te, je re_de_viens mé_lan_co_li_que...
pp pizz. e C. Fag.
p
249
Труффальдино
Trouffaldino
Più mosso.
Король, испугавшись.
Le Roi, effrayé.
accelerando
Ой, какъ
Oh, je
И_ди, и_ди! И_ди ско_рѣ_е!
Partez, par_tez! Par_tez de sui_te!
249
T-ne
f accelerando
Fiati
Più mosso.
ff
Cor.
250 L'istesso tempo (Allegro non troppo).
Труф.
Trouf.
страш_но! какъ страш_но!
trem_ble! je trem_ble!
Выскакиваетъ дьяволъ Фарфарелло съ мѣхами и, припрыгивая, дуетъ Принцу и Труффальдино въ спину.
Apparaît le diable Farfarello avec un soufflet et, sautillant, souffle dans le dos du Prince et de Trouffaldino.
f
T-ni gliss.

Принцъ и Труффальдино стрѣлою вылетаютъ вонъ. Фарфарелло за нимъ.
Le Prince et Trouffaldino partent comme des flèches. Farfarello les poursuit.

251

ff *agitato*

252

ff Cor., Quart.

Король, въ бурномъ отчаяніи. *ff*
Le Roi, farouchement desespéré.

Все ______ по - - гиб - - - - -
Tout ______ *s'é* - - *crou* - - - - -

ff T-ni

253
Падаетъ въ обморокѣ на землю.
Il tombe par terre évanoui.
Король
Roi
ло!
le!
ff Tutti
Панталонъ, въ неподдѣльномъ горѣ.
Pantalon, sincèrement malheureux.
254 Poco meno mosso.
Ка - ко - е
Quel dé - sas - tre
dim. e ritard.
p
Cl.
Пант.
Pant.
се - мей-но-е
pour la fa - mil - le,
и го-су - дар-ствен-но-е
quelle ca-ta - stro - phe
255
Più mosso (Allegro).
Падаетъ рядомъ съ Королемъ.
Il tombe à coté du Roi.
pp
не - сча стье!
pour l'é - tat!
Занавѣсъ.
Rideau.
pizz.
T-be e Tamb. mil.
f
fff Tutti

АКТЪ III.

КАРТИНА I.

Пустыня.

Магъ Челій дѣлаетъ круги, принуждая явиться Фарфарелло.

ACTE III.

TABLEAU I.

Désert.

Le Magicien Tchélio trace des cercles pour forcer Farfarello à apparaître.

259
Чел.
Tchél.
рел - - - ло!
rel - - - lo!
mf
Фар - фа - рел - -
Far - fa - rel - -
f
p
pizz. e Timp.
ло!
lo!
Фар-фа-рел - - ло!
Far-fa-rel - - lo!
f Tutti
3
p
pizz. e Timp.
260
Фар - фа - рел - ло, Фар - фа - рел - ло, Фар - фа-
Far - fa - rel - lo, Far - fa - rel - lo, Far - fa-
fp Col legno, Fag., Ob. c.-al.
fp
рел - - - - - - - - - - - - ло!
rel - - - - - - - - - - - - lo!
f
p

261
Чел.
Tchél.
Фар - фа - рел - ло, Фар - фа - рел - ло, Фар - фа-
Far - fa - rel - lo, Far - fa - rel - lo, Far - fa-
fp
рел - - - - - - - - - - ло!
rel - - - - - - - - - - lo!
f
p
262 Poco più mosso.
Фар - фа - рел - - - - ло, Фар - фа - рел - - - - -
Far - fa - rel - - - - lo, Far - fa - rel - - - - -
Fl.,Cl.
V. I
poco dim.
Celli
Bassi pizz.
263
ло! Фар - фа - рел - - - - - ло, Фар - фа -
lo! Far - fa - rel - - - - - lo, Far - fa -
poco dim.

264
Чел.
Tchél.
ас - - - - - - се - -
рел - - - - - ло! Фар-фа - рел-ло, Фар-фа - рел-ло, Фар-фа -
rel - - - - - lo! Far-fa - rel-lo, Far-fa - rel-lo, Far-fa -
mp
f subito
p
ас - - - - - се -
le - - - - - - ran - - - - do
рел-ло, Фар-фа - рел-ло, Фар-фа - рел-ло, Фар-фа - рел - - - - - -
rel-lo, Far-fa - rel-lo, Far-fa - rel-lo, Far-fa - rel - - - - - -
le
ran
do
ff
Allegro moderato.
265
Появляется Фарфарелло.
Farfarello apparaît.
ло!
lo!
3 T-be, V-ni, V-le, Piatti
ff
6 Cor.
3 T-ni, Celli, Bassi
Фарфарелло
Farfarello
266
f
Ho - là!
Ho - là!
Кто
Qui
3 T-ni, Timp.
T-ni glis. e Fiati
Quart.

Фарф.
Farf.
— зоветъ ме-ня изъ тьмы и у-жа-са?
— m'appelle i-ci du fond des noires té-nèbres?
267
Ты на-сто-я-щій магъ? Иль
Dis, es tu un vrai sor-cier? Ou
fp
Fag. e C. F.
pizz.
только те-а-траль-ный магъ?
bien un sor-cier de thé-âtre?
268 Moderato.
Челій, сдержанно.
Tchélio, réservé.
Я магъ те-а-траль-ный, а так-же на-сто-
Qui, certes, de thé-â-tre. Quand même aus-si un
serioso
C. F. e Tuba
ten.
un poco cresc.

269
Повышая голосъ.
En élevant la voix.
Чел.
Tchél.
я - щій. И о - чень гроз - ный,
vrai sor - cier. Je suis ter - ri - ble,
Bassi, espress.
T-ni
c. sord.
Fag., C. F., Celli pizz.
T-no
270
и о - чень страш - ный. Будь о - сто - ро - женъ,
je suis fé - ro - ce. Eh bien, prends gar - de,
Bassi
Ob. c.-al.
espress.
T-be
271
Фарфарелло
Farfarello
Спраши - вай.
Bien, questionnes.
будь по - слу - шенъ. От - вѣ - чай!
sois do - ci - le. Ré - ponds moi!
Quart. e Timp.
G.P.
G. P.
272
Фарф.
Farf.
Ле - жатъ.
Cou - chés.
Грозно.
Terrible.
От - вѣ - чай мнѣ: гдѣ о - ни?
Dis de sui - te, où sont ils?
pizz.
Quart. e Timp.

273 Нѣсколько иронически.
Légèrement ironique.
Фарф.
Farf.
Я имъ
J'ai souf-
Чел.
Tchél.
По-че-му о-ни ле-жатъ?
Et pour-quoi sont ils cou-chés?
273
Ob. c-al.
mp pizz.
f arco e Cor. con sord.
Cor.
pizz.
дулъ,
flé,
Дуетъ мѣхомъ.
Il souffle avec le soufflet.
souf-flé.
T-ni glis.
274 Poco più mosso.
но мнѣ по-на-до-би-лось въ адъ, и я ихъ бро-силъ.
Mais à l'en-fer j'ai dû des-cendre, et ils tom-bè-rent.
pp
mf T-ni, T-ba, Piatti
pp Quart.
275 Andantino.
Челій, мрачно.
Tchélio, sombre.
Къ Кре-
Chez
Ку-да ты ихъ ду-ешь?
Où mè-ne ton souf-fle?
275 Andantino.
Cor.
p
pesante

276
accelerando
Фарф.
Farf.
он - тѣ въ за_мокъ.
la Cré - on_te.
Чел.
Tchél.
А знаешь ли ты, что тамъ о - ни по -
Mais tu ne sais pas que ce se - ra leur
p Cor. e pizz.
a tempo
Вотъ по - то - му я ихъ и ду - ю.
C'est pour ce - là que je les souf - fle.
гиб - нутъ?
per - te?
f
pp Quart.
277 Più animato.
Дѣлая магическіе жесты, повелительно.
Faisant des gestes magiques, impérieusement.
За - кли_на - ю те_
Je t'or_donne ar - rê - te
V-ni
mp Fag., C.F. e Bassi
T-ba c. sord.
mp
278
бя: о - ста_но_вись! о - ста_но_
toi! ar - rê_te toi! ar - rê - te
mf

Чел.
Tchél.
ff
вись! о - ста - но - вись! За - кли -
toi! ar - rê - te toi! Je t'or -
cresc.
8
ff Tutti
Фарфарелло
Farfarello
279 Moderato.
Насмѣшливо.
Moqueur.
p
Ха-ха-ха - ха-ха-ха-ха-ха - ха! За - пом - ни,
Ha-ha-ha - ha-ha-ha-ha-ha - ha! Mon pau - vre
rit.
на - - ю!
don - - ne!
279 Moderato.
p
Fiati, pizz., Piatti
C. F.
con Ped.
Фарф.
Farf.
280
Магъ: ты проиг - ралъ ихъ въ кар - ты, и по - то - му
vieux, tu as per - du aux car - tes, et pour ce - là
твo - и за - кля - тья не по - мо - гутъ. Про - щай!
tes sor - ti - lèges sont i - nu - ti - les. A - dieu!
Исчезаетъ.
Il disparaît.

Безсильный гнѣвъ Челія.
Fureur stérile de Tchélio.
281
ff veloce
Andante.
Adagio.
T-ni con sord.
p
282
Принцъ и Труффальдино бодро входятъ.
Le Prince et Trouffaldino entrent gaillardement.
Fag.
mp
pizz.
Принцъ
Le Prince
Вѣ-теръ стихъ: зна-читъ а-пель-си-ны близ-ко.
Plus de vent, c'est que les o-ranges sont pro-ches.
Труффальдино
Trouffaldino
По-
A
p
Пр.
Pr.
Не важ-но.
Qu'impor-te!
Труф.
Trouf.
мо-е-му, э-то былъ ци-клонъ.
mon a-vis c'é-tait un cy-clone.
И-ли можетъ быть пас-
Ou ce-la peut être un mous-

283 Allegro.
Пр.
Pr.
Не важ - но.
Qu'im-por - te!
Труф.
Trouf.
сатъ.
son.
Челій, останавливаетъ ихъ.
Tchélio, les retenant.
ff
Ку - да вы, без -
Ar - rê - tez!
Où
Allegro.
283
ff Quart.
284
Пр.
Pr.
И - скать три
Je cherche les
Чел.
Tchél.
ум - ны-е?!
donc allez vous?
284
Fag.
ff
fp
285
Пр.
Pr.
а - пель - си - на.
trois o - ran - ges.
Съ ужасомъ.
Terrifié.
ff
Чел.
Tchél.
Но вѣдь о - ни же
Les trois o - ran - ges?
285
8
f
ff Quart.

Чел.
Tchél.
въ зам - кѣ у Кре - он - ты!
Mais elles sont chez Cré - on - te!
8
286
Принцъ
Le Prince
Я не бо - юсь Кре - он - ты.
Je ne crains pas Cré - on - te.
V. I
p espress.
Fag.
Ob.
p
Fag.
p
287
L'istesso tempo.
Пр.
Pr.
Я не бо -
Une cui - si -
Челій
Tchélio
Но ихъ хра - нитъ у - жас - на - я ку - хар - ка!
Elles sont gar - dées par une ter - rible cui - si - niè - re!
L'istesso tempo.
287
Fl.
Fl.
p

288
Пр.
Pr.
юсь — ку - хар - ки.
niè - re, c'est drô - le!
Ско - рѣ_е, Труффаль_ди - но!
Plus vi_te, Trouffal - di - no!
Отъ ужаса вытаращивая глаза.
Ayant les yeux hors de la tête de frayeur.
Чел.
Tchél.
Но вѣдь ку-
A_vec une
288
V. I
p espress.
Fl.
Cl.
mp
p
289
Люб - лю,
J'a - dore,
хар - ка у - бьетъ васъ су - по - во - ю лож - кой!
lou - che cette fem - me vous tue - ra sur pla - ce!
289
Fl. e Picc.
cresc.
mf
люб - лю, люб - лю три а - пель-
j'a - dore, j'a - dore les trois o -
p

290
Пр.
Pr.
си - - - на!
ran - - - ges!
Я
Je
Челій, дѣлая страшные жесты.
Tchélio, faisant des gestes terrifiés.
Большо-ю мѣд-ной лож кой!
A-vec une louche en cui - - - vre!
Fiati
V-ni
Cor.
dim.
дол - женъ взять три а-пель-си - на.
dois a - voir les trois o - ran - ges.
291
Труффальдино
Trouffaldino
Ой! какъ
Oh! je
Чел.
Tchél.
Лож - кой по лбу — и на мѣ - - - -
Par sa louche elle tue sur pla - - - -
V. I
c. sord.
cresc.
Moderato.
Труф.
Trouf.
страш - но, какъ страш - но!
trem - ble, je trem - ble!
- стѣ! Вы не зна-е-те, ка-ка-я
- ce! Pre - nez gar-de, cet-te louche est
T-ni

292
Рѣшительно.
Décidé.
Пр.
Pr.
Чел.
Tchél.
Я не бо-ю-ся лож-ки! Ско-рѣ-е, Труффаль-
Moi, je ne crains pas la lou-che! Plus vi-te, Trouffal-
лож-ка!
lour-de!
ff
293
ди-но!
di-no!
Видя, что невозможно удержать Принца.
Constatant qu'il est impossible de retenir le Prince.
По-слушай, Труффаль-ди-но...
E-cou-te, Trouffal-di-no...
pp
Cl. bas.
Bassi c. sord.
Cl.
Таинственно.
Mystérieusement.
294
Вотъ на тебѣ волшеб-ный бан-тикъ. Не зна-ю на-вѣр-но-
Em-por-te ce ru-ban ma-gi-que. Peut ê-tre ce ru-ban en
misterioso
pp Quart. con sord., Cl., G. Cassa
Cor. con sord.
pp misterioso
Fl.
Ob.
T-ba
T-be, Cl.
Fag.
е, но мо-жетъ быть онъ по-нра-вит-ся ку-хар-кѣ. Тог-
soie pour-rait bien ra-vir l'af-freu-se cui-si-niè-re. A-
V. I
Cor. con sord.
Ob., T-ba
p

295 Più mosso.
Труффальдино, нацѣпляя бантикъ.
Trouffaldino, s'accrochant le ruban.
Спа - си - бо, доб - рый
Mer - ci, mon Ma - gi -
Чел.
Tchél.
да скорѣй хва - тай - те а - пель - си - ны!
lors de suite sau - tez sur les o - ran - ges!
295 Più mosso.
Cl. e V-ni
Quart., arco e pizz.
p
mf
Ob. c.-al. e pizz.
Принцъ, теряя терпѣніе.
Le Prince, perdant patience.
296
f
Ско - рѣ - е, Труффальди - но!
Plus vi - te, Trouffal - di - no!
Труф.
Trouf.
Магъ.
cien.
Чел.
Tchél.
И пом - ни - те, без - ум - ны - я дѣ - ти:
Sa - chez en - core, en - fants té - mé - rai - res:
V-ni
ten.
296
ten.
p
Quart.
Чел.
Tchél.
ес - ли вамъ до - ста - нут - ся три а - пель - си - на,
si les trois o - ran - ges vous ap - par - tien - nent,
Fag.
p
f
8va bassa

297
poco rit.
Чел.
Tchél.
от-кры-вать-ихъ мож-но толь-ко близъ во-ды,
qu'el-les soient-ou-ver-tes près d'une sour-ce d'eau,
Cor., T-ni, Timp.
298 Poco meno mosso.
Принцъ
Le Prince
a piacere
О, сла-дост-
Je rê-ve
и-на-че бу-детъ го-ре.
si-non, je vois un dra-me.
Fag.
Пр.
Pr.
ны-е а-пель-си-ны!
de mes chères o-ran-ges!
Про-
A-
Труффальдино
Trouffaldino
Спа-си-бо, доб-рый Магъ!
Mer-ci, mon Ma-gi-cien!
Allegro non troppo.
299
Выскакиваетъ Фарфарелло съ мѣхами. Принцъ и Труффальдино стрѣлою вылетаютъ вонъ. Фарфарелло за ними.
Farfarello bondit sur la scène avec son soufflet. Le Prince et Trouffaldino s'envolent comme des flèches. Farfarello les poursuit.
щай!
dieu!
3 T-be
Celli, Bas., Fag., C. F.
T-ni glis.

300
ff Tutti
Челій, заклинаетъ имъ вслѣдъ.
Tchélio, faisant des incantations dans leur direction.
301
ff
Да ми - ну - етъ
Que le sort les
Чел.
Tchél.
васъ страш - на - я лож - - - - ка!
garde con - tre la lou - - - - che!
6 Cor.
Занавѣсъ.
Rideau.
302 Allegro con brio.
6 Cor.

V.I.
p
Celli pizz. e Fag.
m.d.
m.s.
Cl. e pizz.
303
V.I.
mf
T-be con sord.
p
mfp
Fl., Ob., pizz.
304
V.I.
cresc.
mf
T-be con sord.
p
mfp
Fl., Ob., pizz.

305
306
307
308
cresc.
mf
f
Cor. glis.
T-be, V-ni
Cor.
mp
Cor., pizz., Xyl.
cresc.
ff
Cor. glis.
T-be, V-ni
Cor.
mp
cresc.
f

più facile
f
ff
309
T-ni
f
ff
p
m.d.
m.s.
Cl.e pizz.
310
V.I
mf
T-be con.sord.
p
mfp
cresc.
mf
Занавѣсъ.
Rideau.
f T-ni glis.

КАРТИНА II.
Дворъ замка Креонты.

TABLEAU II.
La cour du château de Créonte.

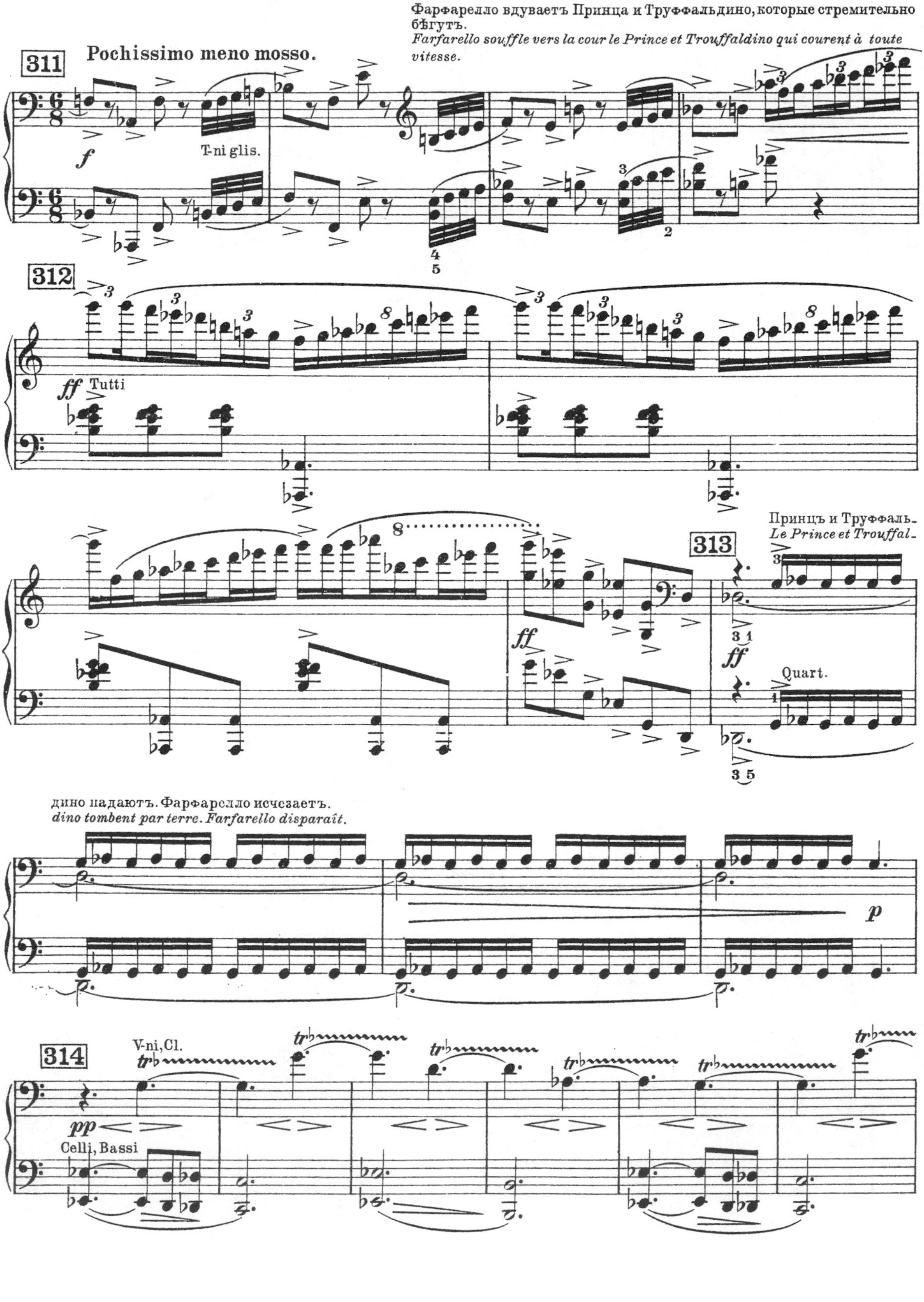

Фарфарелло вдуваетъ Принца и Труффальдино, которые стремительно бѣгутъ.
Farfarello souffle vers la cour le Prince et Trouffaldino qui courent à toute vitesse.

311 **Pochissimo meno mosso.**

f

T-ni glis.

312

ff Tutti

ff

313

Принцъ и Труффаль-
Le Prince et Trouffal-

ff

Quart.

дино падаютъ. Фарфарелло исчезаетъ.
dino tombent par terre. Farfarello disparaît.

p

314

V-ni, Cl.

pp

Celli, Bassi

315
Принцъ, приподнимаясь.
Le Prince, se relevant.
Гдѣ мы?
Qu'est-ce?
Труффальдино
Trouffaldino
Бо-юсь по-ду-мать...
J'ai peur, mon Prince...
316
Видятъ большую вывѣску на замкѣ и читаютъ по складамъ.
Ils voient une grande enseigne sur le château et lisent en épelant.
Кре...
Cré...
V-ni
pp agitato
Пр.
Pr.
Труф.
Trouf.
он...
on...
та...
te...
cresc.
Timp. e T. mil.
317
Вскакиваютъ въ безумномъ страхѣ.
Ils se relèvent vivement, pris d'une terreur folle.
Ахъ! ка-кі-е у-жа-сы!
Ah! c'est ef-fro-ya-ble!
Ахъ! ка-кі-е у-жа-сы!
Ah! c'est ef-fro-ya-ble!
Tutti
f feroce
Celli, Bassi, Fag.

318 Più mosso (Vivo).
Пр.
Pr.
И въ самомъ дѣ-лѣ страш - но!
Cette fois c'est ef-fro - ya - ble!
Труф.
Trouf.
По - гиб - ли мы!
La mort ar-rive!
V. I
fp
poco cresc.
319
По - стой. Нѣтъ,
At - tends. Non,
Уй - дем - те, Принцъ... уй-демъ ско-рѣ - е.
Par - tons, mon Prince... par-tons bien vi - te.
mf
dim.
pp
320
нѣтъ. Мы долж-ны до-стать три а-пель-си - на.
non. Nous de-vons a-voir les trois o-ran - ges.
cresc.
f

321
Пр.
Pr.
Страш - но...
Ter-ri - - ble...
Слу - шай,
Tché - lio,
Труф.
Trouf.
Ой, какъстраш-но!
C'est ter - ri - ble!
Страш - - - - но...
Ter- - - - - ri - ble...
dim.
pp
Труффальдино, какъ буд-то Магъ ска - залъ, что мы долж -
il me semble, a dit qu'il faut cher - cher les trois o -
322
ны и - скатьихъ на кух - - - - нѣ? На
ran - ges dans la cui - si - - - - ne? Est-ce
На кух - нѣ.
C'est jus - te.
mp

323
Пр.
Pr.
кух - нѣ?
jus - te?
Вотъ здѣсь кух - ня.
Voi - là la por - te.
Труф.
Trouf.
На кух - нѣ.
C'est jus - te.
323
dim.
pp
Крадутся къ кухнѣ.
Ils se glissent vers la cuisine.
pp
324
Принцъ
Le Prince
Труффальдино
Trouffaldino
О, сла - - - дост -
Je rê - - - ve
Принцъ, бе - ре - ги - тесь ку - хар - ки!
Prince, mé - fiez vous de la lou - che!
324
f
dim.
p
f
325
Пр.
Pr.
ны - е а - пель - си - - ны!
de mes chères o - ran - - ges!
Труф.
Trouf.
Принцъ... Принцъ... тамъ
Prince... Prince... je
325
dim.
pp
pp

Восторженно.
Extasié.
Пр.
Pr.
А - пель - си - - - - - ны!
Les o - ran - - - - - ges!
Труф.
Trouf.
страшная кухарка!
crains la cuisinière!
Она убьетъ насъ суповою ложкой!
Elle nous tuera avec sa grande louche!
p
mf
326
А - пель - си
Les o - ran
mp
f
327 Meno mosso.
ны!
ges!
Кухарка съ грохотомъ трясетъ изнутри дверью.
La cuisinière avec fracas secoue la porte du côté intérieur.
Отскакиваютъ.
Ils reculent en bondissant.
ff
А!
Ah!
Трясетъ опять.
La porte est secouée de nouveau.
ff Cor, T-ni, G. Cas., Timp.

Пр.
Pr
Труф.
Trouf.
Смерть на_ша!
C'est el_le!
Ги_ бель на_ша!
Ah! c'est el_le!
gliss.
Arpa
328
Опрометью бросаются отъ кухни и прячутся въ разныя стороны.
Ils fuient éperdument de la porte de la cuisine et se cachent dans des endroits différents.
Quart. e 3 Cl.
T-be, Cor. con sord.
(senza rit.)
Moderato.
329
Дверь настежь, и появляется кухарка съ огромной ложкой.
La porte s'ouvre toute grande, et la cuisinière apparaît avec une énorme louche.
Cor.
Tuba solo
Celli, Bassi
Кухарка, хриплымъ басомъ.
La Cuisinière, d'une voix de basse enrouée.
330
Осматривается; громче.
Regardant autour d'elle;
d'une voix plus forte.
Кто тутъ пи_щитъ?
Qui piaille i_ci?
Я го_во_рю: кто
Je veux sa_voir: qui
Tuba
T-ni e Timp.

331 Meno mosso.
Кух.
Cuis.
— тутъ пи - щитъ?
— piaille i - ci?
Не получивъ отвѣта направляется впередъ, осматриваясь по сторонамъ.
Ne recevant pas de réponse; elle s'avance inspectant de tous côtés.
Най - ду,
Sor - tez!
Tuba
etc.
C. Fag.
най-ду.
Sor-tez!
Все рав-но най - ду.
Je trouverai sans faute.
Все рав-но най - ду.
Je trouverai sans faute.
Allegro.
332 Находитъ Труффальдино.
Elle découvre Trouffaldino.
Ахъ,
Ah,
Tuba
Cl.
Ob. c.-al. e Tuba
Piatti
Ob., T-be con sord.
Труффальдино, безъ памяти отъ ужаса, стонетъ.
Trouffaldino, perdant presque la conscience de frayeur, gémit.
rit.
А!—
Ah!—
А!—
Ah!—
О!—
Oh!—
ты, ще-нокъ!
toi, vau-rien!
Cl.
rit.

333 Andantino.
334 Allegro moderato.
Труф.
Trouf.
Ахъ...
Ah...
Возмущенно.
Révoltée.
Кух.
Cuis.
Ка-ковъ ще-нокъ:
Quel sale vau-rien:
ку-да за-брал-ся!
une telle au-da-ce!
Cl.,Fl.
Tuba
T-ni e Timp.
я... ку-хар-ка...
moi... ma-da-me...
poco rit.
ку-ха-роч-ка...
ma belle da-me...
Ob. e Celli vibrato
335 Poco meno mosso.
Не на-до... ку-ха-
Ma-da-me... ma no-
Кухарка
La Cuisinière
Да я те-бя за но-ги, и бро-шу въ печь!
At-tends, vo-leur, je te jette dans le four-neau!
Fl. e Pic.
Quart.
f feroce
V-ni

Труф.
Trouf.
- роч - ка...
- ble dame...
Кух.
Cuis.
Да я те - бя лож - кой по лбу и
A - vec ma louche je t'é - cra - se et te
Quart.
p
f feroce
Tuba
f Quart.
336
Più mosso.
Я здѣсь слу... слу -
Je suis ve... ve -
въгрязно - е ве ро!
flanque dans les or - dures!
V. I e Fl.
p
pp
чай - но... по о - шиб - кѣ...
nu là... par mé - gar - de...
337
Пытается бѣжать.
Il essaie de s'enfuir.
Quart., Cl.
f precipitato
Кухарка взмахиваетъ ложкой и, поймавъ его за шиворотъ, немилосердно трясетъ.
La cuisinière brandit la louche et, attrappant Trouffaldino au collet, le secoue sans pitié.
f

338
Кухарка
La Cuisinière
Ку - да?
Co - quin!
ff 3 Cl.
Tuba.
f col legno e Fag.
Кух.
Cuis.
Бѣжать?
Tu fuis?
Всю ду - шу вы - тря - су.
Je te f'rai ren - dre l'âme.
Возмущенно.
Révoltée.
rit.
На кух - ню лѣ - зетъ!
Vio - ler ma cui - si - ne!
Tuba
f col legno e Cor. con sord.
rit.
339
Moderato.
Вдругъ замѣчаетъ волшебный бантикъ и сразу заинтересовывается.
Tout à coup elle apperçoit le ruban magique. Elle est immédiatement interessée par lui.
più p
Что э - то та - ко - е у те -
Qu'est ce que tu portes sur ton cos -
pp Quart.
Fl. Solo
mp
Труффальдино, еще не приходя въ себя.
Trouffaldino, qui n'est pas encore d'aplomb.
Бан - тикъ...
Un ru - ban...
Несмѣло.
Timidement.
Не - у - же - ли... хо - ро - шій?
A - do - ra - ble? Tu trou - ves?
Смягчая тонъ.
D'une voix plus douce.
бя?
tume?
Бан - тикъ?
Fich - tre!
Ка - кой хо - ро - шій бан - тикъ!
Mais il est a - do - ra - ble!
p pizz. e Cl.

340
Кух.
Cuis.
За-мѣ-ча-тель-но прі-ят-ный бан-тикъ. От-ку-да онъ у те-бя?
Ce pe-tit ru-ban fait perdre la tê-te! Qui t'a don-né ce ru-ban?
T-be
p arco e Fag.
mp
mf
Tuba
Труффальдино, начиная смѣлѣть.
Trouffaldino, s'enhardissant.
Видишь ли... ку-ха-роч-ка... э-то... се-кретъ...
Ça, vois-tu... com-ment te dire?... C'est un... se-cret...
Вотъ какъ? Се-
Tiens, tiens! Vrai-
Ob.
espress.
Cl.
Fag.
p
341
Allegro.
Принцъ большими беззвучными прыжками направляется къ кухнѣ и скрывается въ ней.
Le Prince par de grands bonds silencieux se dirige vers la cuisine et y disparaît.
кретъ!
ment?
V. II con sord.
pp
Fl. e V. I con sord.
pp
А бан-тикъ въ са-момъ дѣ-лѣ о-чень
Ja-mais je n'ai trou-vé une telle mer-

Кух.
Cuis.
ми - лый.
veil - le.
Ты бы мнѣ е -
Ne vou - drais tu
cresc.
Принцъ появляется изъ кухни съ тремя огромными, въ человѣческую голову, апельсинами и большими прыжками спасается за ворота замка.
Le Prince sort de la cuisine avec trois énormes oranges de la dimension d'une tête d'homme et par de grands bonds disparaît derrière la porte du château.
342
го не по - да - рилъ?
pas m'en faire ca - deau?
А?
Eh?
Fl., Picc., T-be c.sord.
mp
Кокетливо.
Avec coquetterie.
На память...
Pour me plai - re...
p
Celli e Fag.
343
Труффальдино
Trouffaldino
А те -
C'est pour
assai rit.
На па - мять...
Pour me plai - re...
V. I pizz.
ritard.
p a tempo

poco rit.
Труф.
Trouf.
бѣ е - го хо - тѣ - лось бы и - мѣть отъ ме - ня на па - мять?
te rappe - ler de moi que tu le veux, en es - tu bien sû - re?
poco rit.
344
Moderato.
Принцъ, высовывая голову изъ-за воротъ.
Le Prince, passant la tête par la porte.
Труф.фаль - ди - но... Труф.фальдино...
Trouf - fal - di - no... Trouf - fal - di - no...
Торжественно вручая бантикъ.
Lui remettant pompeusement le ruban.
Такъ вотъ возь - ми и
Prends le et sois con -
Кухарка
La Cuisinière
Да ужъ хо - тѣ - лось бы.
Ça me fe - rait plai - sir.
2 Fag.
Tuba
pizz.
Труф.
Trouf.
пом - ни.
ten - te.
345
Держа передъ собою бантикъ, восторженно.
La cuisinière, charmée, regarde le ruban.
Кух.
Cuis.
Чуд - - - -
O, ______
T-be, Cor. con sord.
Quart.
Cor. e Cl.
pesante
mp espress.
Bassi

Труффальдино убѣгаетъ.
Trouffaldino s'enfuit.
Кух.
Cuis.
— ный, без - по - доб - ный бан - тикъ!
— ru - ban in - com - pa - ra - ble!
Не спуская глазъ съ бантика, шаритъ рукой по тому мѣсту, гдѣ былъ Труффальдино.
346
Fixant toujours le ruban, cherche Trouffaldino en tâtonnant vers l'endroit où il était.
Ласково.
Caressante.
Занавѣсъ.
Rideau.
Ну, гдѣ же ты?
Où donc es - tu?
Гдѣ ты тутъ?
Que fais - tu?
Маль - чон - ка...
P'tit dia - ble!...
3 Clar.
pizz. e Tuba
G.P.
Celli, Bassi
347
Allegro con brio.
cresc.
dim.
348
V. I
Celli pizz. e Fag.
m.d.
m.s.
Cl. e pizz.

349
V.I
p T-be con sord.
mfp
cresc.
mf
Fl., Ob., pizz.
350
V.I
p T-be con sord.
mfp
cresc.
mf
Fl., Ob., pizz.
351
8
f
T-be, V-ni
Cor.
352
mp
cresc.
Cor., pizz., Xyl.

353
8
ff
Cor.
gliss.
T-be,V-ni
Cor.
354
mp
cresc.
f
T-ni
più facile
f
ff
355
f
ff
p
m.d.
m.s.
Cl. e pizz.

356
V. I
p
T-be con sord.
mf
mf
p
357
cresc.
mf
p
Fag. e Celli, pizz.
Cl. e Arpa
pp
Занавѣсъ.
Rideau.

КАРТИНА III.

Пустыня.

Декорація первой картины того же акта. Вечеръ. Принцъ и Труффальдино медленно входятъ съ противоположной, чѣмъ въ I картинѣ, стороны, таща за собою на веревкѣ три апельсина, которые выросли до такой степени, что внутри каждаго, можетъ помѣститься человѣкъ.

TABLEAU III.

Désert.

Le décor du 1er tableau de ce même acte. C'est le soir. Le Prince et Trouffaldino entrent lentement du côté opposé à celui par lequel ils entrèrent au 1er tableau. Ils traînent derrière eux avec une corde trois oranges qui ont grandi à tel point que chacune peut contenir une personne.

360
Pochissimo più mosso.
Принцъ
Le Prince
Я спать хо-чу!
Ah, quel sommeil!
Труф.
Trouf.
Я пить хо-чу!
Ah, quel le soif!
360
Pochissimo più mosso.
V.I, Cl.
Picc., Fl., Arpe
Пр.
Pr.
Я такъ у-сталъ!
Je suis bri-sé!
Я
J'ai
V-ni e Cl.
Picc., Fl., Arpe
361
Я за-
Je vou-
такъ жа-жду!
soif, Prin-ce!
361
V. I
Cor.

Пр.
Pr.
poco rit.
сну не - мно - го, Труф-фаль - ди - но.
drais m'é - ten - dre, Trouf - fal - di - no.
V. II
pp
una corda
poco rit.
T-be con sord.
362
Труффальдино, взволнованно.
Trouffaldino, agité.
rit.
Принцъ, но по-ка вы бу-де-те спать, я у-мру отъ жа-жды!
Prince! mais pen-dant que vous dor-mi-rez, je mour-rai de soif!
col legno, Cl., Fag.
subito f
V-ni e Fl.
p espress. e rit.
G. P.
tre corde
363
Moderato.
Принцъ
Le Prince
Ни-че-го, от-дох-немъ, мы тог-да пой-демъ бод-рѣ-е. Ло-
Ce n'est rien, dors un peu, le som-meil donne-ra des for-ces. Couche
p Quart. e Cl. bas.
C.F.
Ложится и засыпаетъ.
Il se couche et s'endort.
364
Пр.
Pr.
жи-ся, Труффаль-ди-но.
toi, bon Trouf-fal-di-no.
Fl., Ob.
Allegro.
p Arpa
Cor.
pp Celli, Bassi, Fag.

Труффальдино
Trouffaldino

365

Какъ мо-гу——— я спать, ког-да ме - ня сжи-га-етъ жа - жда?
Il est drôle,——— le Prince! Dor-mir, quand j'ai une soif de dia - ble!

mf

Труф. *Trouf.*

А во-кругъ——— нѣтъ ни кап - ли во-ды.
Im-pos-sible——— de trou-ver une gout-te d'eau.

ten.

V. I V. II V. I

366

Труф. *Trouf.*

f

Дай - те же мнѣ пить!
Don - nez moi à boire!

V-le

f

Труф. *Trouf.*

Дай - те мнѣ во - ды!
Don - nez moi de l'eau!

V. II

Cor.

f

Cor.

367
Труф.
Trouf.
Дай - те же ско - рѣ - - - - е!
Don - nez m'en de sui - - - te!
V. I
f
Cl.
Cor.
T-be, Fl.
sf
368
Принцъ! Принцъ!
Prince! Prince!
f pizz. e Fiati.
Про-сни-тесь, про-сни-тесь! Ахъ... Принцъ...
Mon Prin-ce! Le-vez vous, Prince! Prince... Ah!..
poco rit.
369
Meno mosso (Allegro moderato).
370
Онъ спитъ, какъ глу-хой.
Il dort comme un sourd.
Arpa
G. P.
p
pizz.
V-ni
pp dolce
3T-be con sord.

Останавливается передъ апельсинами.
S'arrêtant devant les oranges.
371
Труф.
Trouf.
А - пель - си - ны?...
Les o - ran - ges?...
Вотъ ес - ли бы рас -
Mais si j'ouv - rais ne
V-le pizz.
G. P.
p
Fag.
крыть о - динъ изъ нихъ...
fut-ce qu'une seule des trois?
372
Онъ дол - женъ
Elles sont si
3 T-be con sord.
mp
3 T-ni
mfp
быть та - кимъ соч - нымъ!
belles et si ju - teu - ses!
mp espress.
p
373
Meno mosso.
Берется за мечъ, но сейчасъ же отскакиваетъ отъ апельсина.
Il saisit son glaive, mais immédiatement recule de l'orange.
Нѣтъ! что ска - жетъ Принцъ?
Non! j'ai peur du Prince!
p Ob. c-al.
p Celli pizz.
p

374
Allegro.
Труф.
Trouf.
А ес - ли я у - мру? У - мру сей - часъ отъ э - той
Et si j'al - lais mou - rir, mou - rir de soif a - vant qu'on
pp Celli, Bassi, Fag.
375
жа - жды? Вѣдь тог - да Принцъ не до - не - сетъ ни
m'ai - de? A - lors le Prince ne pour - ra ja - mais traî -
ten.
V. I
V. II
mf
376
од - но - го. И все по -
ner tout seul. Et tout s'é -
f
p pizz. e Fiati
377
гиб - нетъ: и а - пель - си - ны, и Принцъ, и я.
crou - le: les trois o - ran - ges, le Prince et moi.
T-be c. sord.
cresc.

Труф.
Trouf.
Нѣтъ, ужъ луч-ше пусть я съѣмъ о-динъ.
C'est vrai-ment plus sage que j'en mange une.
mp
Cor.
pizz. e Ob. c.-al.
378
Pochissimo più largamente.
Въ восторгѣ обнимаетъ апельсинъ.
Extasié, il embrasse une orange.
Соч - - - - - - - ный а - пель -
Qu'elle est donc ju -
Arpe, Cor. gliss., Quart., Fiati.
379
синъ!
teu - - - - - - - - se!
Круп - - - - - - ный а - пель -
Ah, qu'elle est é -

380
Труф.
Trouf.
синъ!
norme!
Ped.
Ped.
381
Распиливаетъ мечомъ апельсинъ.
Il scie l'orange en deux parties avec son glaive.
f Quart., Fiati
Изъ апельсина появляется дѣвушка въ бѣломъ.
De l'orange sort une jeune fille en blanc.
ff Cor., Tuba, Piatti
382
Meno mosso.
Moderato.
Линетта, сiяя.
Linette, rayonante.
Я Прин_цес_са Ли_нет_та.
Je suis la Prin_ces_se Li_net_te.
Труффальдино, пораженъ.
Trouffaldino, bouleversé.
Бѣ_ла_я дѣ_вуш_ка?
Une jeu_ne fille en blanc?
382
Meno mosso.
Moderato.
Ob., Camp.
p pizz. e Timp.
G.P.
Cor.
383
Più mosso.
Труф.
Trouf.
Прин_цес_са... вмѣ_сто... а_пель_син_на_го со_ка?..
Prin_ces_se... au lieu... du jus frais d'une o_range?..
Fl., Arpe, Camp.
col legno e Fag.

384
Andantino.
Линетта
Linette
f
Дай мнѣ пить! Дай пить ско-рѣ-е, иль я у-мру от
Donne à boire! A boire, de grâ-ce, si-non je meurs de
Quart., Ob., Fag.
fp
385
Лин.
Lin.
poco rit.
жа-жды, отъ же-сто-кой жа-жды, отъ смер-тель-ной жа-жды!
sui-te. J'ai une soif af-freu-se, j'ai une soif mor-tel-le!
colla parte
pp
p
cresc.
mf
386
Pochissimo più mosso.
Труффальдино, растерянно.
Trouffaldino, désemparé.
Прин-цес-са... Прин-цес-са... гдѣ же мы до-ста-немъ? Вокругъ пу-сты-ня...
Prin-ces-se... Prin-ces-se... où trou-ver une sour-ce? Tout est a-ri-de...
Quart.
p molto ritmato
387
Линетта
Linette
poco rit.
Ско-рѣ-е, ско-рѣ-е! Дай мнѣ пить, без-сер-деч-ный ти-
De grâ-ce, plus vi-te, donne à boire, ne sois pas sans pi-
Труф.
Trouf.
Ахъ, Прин-цес-са...
Oh, Prin-ces-se...
387
Celli espress.
p
mf
poco rit.

388
Лин.
Lin.
ранъ!
tié!
Безрезультатно пытаясь разбудить Принца.
Essayant, sans y parvenir, de réveiller le Prince.
Дай мнѣ хоть кап - лю...
Rien qu'u - ne gout - te...
Труф.
Trouf.
Принцъ, проснитесь!
Prince... mon Prin-ce...
Принцесса... сейчасъ... я от-
Princes-se... Princesse... tout de
V. I
Арра
gliss.
m.s.
pp mf p espress.
m.d.
Celli e Bassi
mf
389
Хоть кап - лю...
A boi - re...
Распиливаетъ мечомъ.
Il scie avec le glaive.
крою другой а-пель-синъ.
suite j'ou-vri - rai l'autre o - range.
p Quart. sul pontic.
f Quart. e Fiati
390
Изъ апельсина выходитъ вторая дѣвушка въ бѣломъ.
De l'orange sort une seconde jeune fille en blanc.
Хоть кап - лю...
A boi - re...
Хоть кап-лю...
Une gout-te...
Какъ, е - ще од - на прин-цес-са?
Quoi, en - core une autre prin-ces - se?
f T-ni, Cor., Piatti
p pizz. e Timp.

Andante assai.
Николетта, сіяя.
Nicolette, rayonnante.
391 Andantino.
Я Принцесса Николетта. Дай мнѣ пить!
Je me nomme Nicolette. Donne à boire!
Лин.
Lin.
Одну лишь
Une seule
Труф.
Trouf.
Что за чудо!
Quel miracle!
Andante assai.
Fl., Arpa, Camp.
391 Andantino.
Quart., Ob., Fag.
Camp., Fl. e Cor. con sord.
Quart.
Ник.
Nic.
Дай пить скорѣе, иль я умру
A boire, de grâce, si non je meurs
Лин.
Lin.
каплю! Въ глазахъ мутится... Спаси меня!
goutte! Ma vue se trouble... Ah, sauve moi!
392
poco rit.
Ник.
Nic.
отъ жажды, отъ жестокой жажды, отъ смер-
de suite. J'ai une soif affreuse, j'ai une
Лин.
Lin.
Спаси... Спаси, спа-
Pitié! O, sauve,
Труффальдино, растерянно отступаетъ передъ обѣими Принцессами, которыя какъ тѣни тянутся за нимъ.
Trouffaldino, effaré, recule devant les deux Princesses qui se tendent vers lui comme des ombres.
Принцессы... стерпите... стерпите хоть
Princesses... patience... seulement quelques
392
poco rit.

393
Ник.
Nic.
тель - ной жа - жды!
soif mor - tel - le!
Въ гла - захъ му -
Ma vue se
Лин.
Lin.
си ме - ня!
sau - ve moi!
Лишь
A
Труф.
Trouf.
f a parte
сут-ки... хоть сут-ки...
heu-res!.. Cou-ra-ge!..
Ахъ, мнѣ
Ah, que
393
V. I, Fl.
Ob.
mf
espress.
mp
f
dim.
T-be e Quart.
394
Ник.
Nic.
тит - ся...
trou - ble...
Спа - си ме-ня...
Pi - tié pour moi...
Упавъ на землю, но продолжая тянуться къ Труффальдино.
Etant déjà parterre elle continue à se tendre vers Trouffaldino.
Умираетъ.
Elle meurt.
Лин.
Lin.
кап-лю!
boi-re!
Сжалься... сжалься... сжаль - ся...
Grâ-ce... grâ-ce... grâ - ce...
Труф.
Trouf.
боль-но ви-дѣть ихъ!
c'est af - freux tout ça!
У-мер-ла?!
Est-elle morte?!
394
Cor. con sord.
p
mfp
mf
Quart., Fiati, Tam. mil.

395
Падаетъ на землю.
Elle tombe.
Шопотомъ.
Murmurant.
Ник.
Nic.
Спа - си...
De l'eau...
каплю...
grâ - ce...
сжалься...
grâ - ce...
сжалься...
grâ - ce...
Arpe e Fl.
pp V. II e V-le sul ponticello
396
Умираетъ.
Elle meurt.
Труффальдино
Trouffaldino
397 Allegro.
И э - та?
En - co - re?
T-be
pp
p
C. F., pizz. e G. Cas.
p
Въ суевѣрномъ страхѣ.
Pris d'une terreur superstitieuse.
Убѣгаетъ.
Il s'enfuit.
Труф.
Trouf.
Бѣжать...
Par - tir...
бѣжать
partir
ско - рѣ - е!
au plus vi - te!
Fiati e col legno
mp
T-be
cresc.
398
V-le
f
dim.

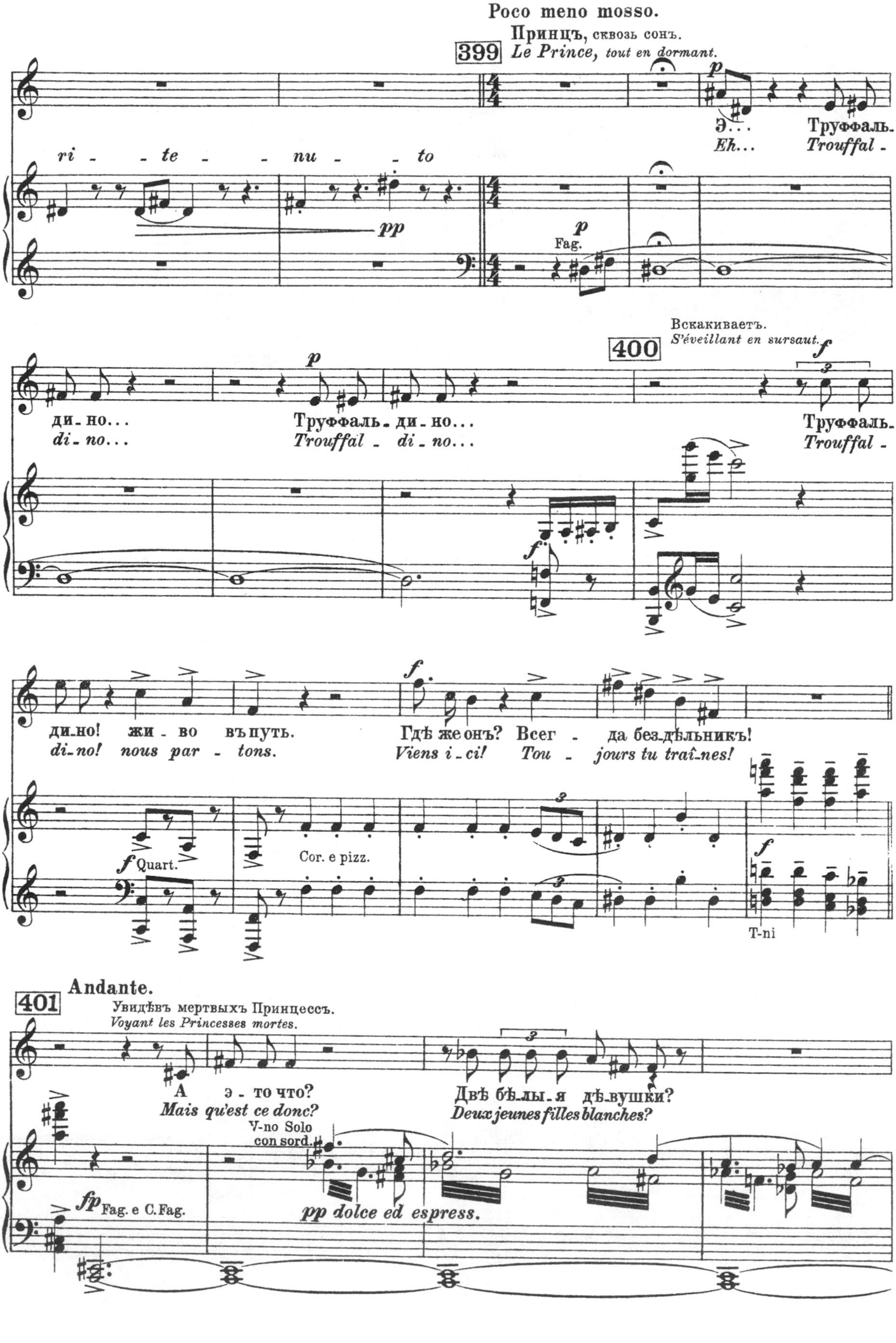

Poco meno mosso.
Принцъ, сквозь сонъ.
399
Le Prince, tout en dormant.
ri - te - nu - to
pp
Fag.
Э... Труффаль-
Eh... Trouffal-
Пр.
Pr.
ди-но... Труффаль-ди-но...
di-no... Trouffal - di-no...
Вскакиваетъ.
400
S'éveillant en sursaut.
Труффаль-
Trouffal-
ди-но! живо въ путь. Гдѣ же онъ? Всег - да без-дѣльникъ!
di-no! nous par - tons. Viens i-ci! Tou - jours tu traînes!
Quart.
Cor. e pizz.
T-ni
401
Andante.
Увидѣвъ мертвыхъ Принцессъ.
Voyant les Princesses mortes.
А э-то что? Двѣ бѣ-лы-я дѣ-вушки?
Mais qu'est ce donc? Deux jeunes filles blanches?
V-no Solo
con sord.
fp Fag. e C.Fag.
pp dolce ed espress.

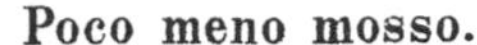

Пр.
Pr.
pp
poco rit.
402 a tempo
Двѣ мертвы-я дѣвушки?
Deux jeunes filles mortes?
Од-нѣ среди пу-сты-ни.
Dans ce dé-sert a-ri-de.
Ка-
E-
T-be con sord.
colla parte
p
p Fiati
Fag. e C.F.
ка-я судьба...
tran-ge des-tin...
403 Tempo di Marcia energica (Allegro moderato).
Четыре солдата маршируютъ черезъ сцену съ преувеличенной военной выправкой.
Quatre soldats entrent en scène avec une allure militaire exagérée.
Celli e Ob. c.-al.
G. P.
mf
Fag.
T-ni, C. F., Bassi e T. mil.
f
Стой-те!
Hal-te!
Солдаты останавливаются, какъ вкопанные.
Les soldats s'arrêtent comme figés sur place.
mf
f
404 Andante.
p
Возьми-те э-тихъ дѣ-вушекъ
Prenez ces deux ca-dav-res
и по-хо-ро-ни-те ихъ.
et en-terrez les là bas.
V-ni, Fl. Arpe
m.s.
pp
rit. assai
pp

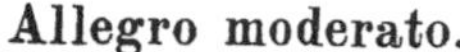

Allegro moderato.

Солдаты рѣзкими военными движеніями направляются къ Принцессамъ и поднимаютъ ихъ.
Les soldats avec des mouvements militaires brusques s'approchent des Princesses et les relèvent de la terre.

405

Celli e Ob. c.-al. *f* V-le Fl. *pp* Cl.

V-le

Неся Принцессъ, маршируютъ въ противоположную кулису.
Portant les Princesses, ils partent par la coulisse opposée à celle par laquelle ils sont entrés.

pp Cl. bas.

406

Fag. *mp* Celli, Bassi, C.F. Tamb. mil.

Cl. bas. *pp* pizz. *senza rit.* *pp*

407 Meno mosso.

Принцъ
Le Prince

408

А-пель-синъ? Я радъ, что на-ко-
Chère o-range... En-fin j'ai le bon-

Cor. *f* Arpa glissando *f* Cor. e Quart.

Пр.
Pr.

нецъ мы о-ста-лись вдво-емъ: а-пель-синъ и я.
heur d'ê-tre seul a-vec toi. Rien que toi et moi!

pizz. T-ni e T-ba *f*

409
Пр.
Pr.
По-ра мнѣ знать, что онъ въ себѣ та - итъ. Я
Je dois sa - voir ce que contient l'o - range. En
Ob.
V. I
mf
pp
зна - ю, въ немъ со-кры - то мо - е сча - стье.
el - le, je le sais, se cache mon rê - ve.
f
410 Poco meno mosso.
А - пельсинъ! А - пельсинъ! От - дай мнѣ мо - е
Chère o-range! Chère o-range! Donne moi ce que je
Quart., Fl., Arpa
f espress.
сча - стье!
cher - che!
411
Съ размаха разрубаетъ мечомъ апельсинъ.
D'un seul coup de glaive il partage l'orange.
Появляется третья бѣлая дѣвушка.
Apparait une troisième jeune fille en blanc.
ff
G. P.
p Ob. c.-al.

412 Andante.
Нинетта
Ninette
p dolce
Да, я Прин-цес-са Ни-нет - - - - - -
Moi, je m'ap-pel-le Ni-net - - - - - -
Пр.
Pr.
p
Принцес-са?!
Princes-se?!
Andante.
412
Арра
pp
Fl., Cl., Cor. con sord., Camp.
G. P.
pp Quart.
Ped.
Ped.
413 Moderato (Passionato e maestoso).
Нин.
Nin.
та!
te!
Падаетъ на колѣни.
Tombant à genoux.
Пр.
Pr.
Прин - цес - са, Прин - цес - са, я и - щу те - бя по все-
Prin - ces - se, Prin - ces - se, je te cherche de-puis que je
413 Moderato (Passionato e maestoso).
Celli espress.
f
Bassi, Fag. e Arpa
ben tenuto
Пр.
Pr.
rit.
a tempo
му— мi-ру! Прин-цес - са, Прин - цес - са, я люб-лю те-бя боль-
suis au mon-de! Prin - ces - se, Prin - ces - se, je t'a - do - re bien plus—
f
rit.
a tempo

Нинетта
Ninette
414 Meno mosso.
p dolce
rit.
Принцъ, я жду те-бя дав-но.
Je t'at-tends de-puis tou-jours.
Въ упоенiи обнимаетъ ея колѣни.
Le Prince, ivre d'amour, lui embrasse les genoux.
Пр.
Pr.
rit.
— ше все-го мi-ра!
— que tout au monde!
О, мо-е сча-стье!
Ah, que je t'a-do-re!
414 Meno mosso.
Fl., Cl.
V. I
rit.
pp
rit. pp
415 Andantino.
Нин.
Nin.
f
Дай мнѣ пить! Дай пить ско-рѣ-е, иль я у-
Donne à boire! A boire, de grâ-ce, si-non je
V-no Solo con sord.
fp Quart., Ob., Ob. c-al.
mf molto espress. e dolente mp
Ob.
Fag.
416
rit.
мру — отъ жажды, отъ же-сто-кой жа-жды, отъ смер-
meurs — de sui-te. J'ai une soif af-freu-se, j'ai une
p
pp
p
mp
cresc. e rit.
Fag., Ob., Quart.

a tempo
417
Нин.
Nin.
тель - ной жа - жды!
soif mor - tel - le!
Хоть кап - лю...
A boi - re!
Принцъ
Le Prince
Прин - цес - са, по - до - жди не - мно - го!
At - tends quel - ques ins - tants, Prin - ces - se!
Здѣсь
C'est
a tempo
mf
dim.
espress. e dolente
Quart.
p
Celli, molto espress.
Въ гла - захъ му - тит - ся...
Ma vue se trou - ble...
Я сла -
Je suc -
Пр.
Pr.
гад - ка - я пу - сты - ня.
un dé - sert ter - ri - ble.
Но мы сей - часъ же от - пра - вим - ся
Mais nous par - tons tout de sui - te en
p
rit.
Падаетъ на руки Принца.
Elle tombe dans les bras du Prince.
бѣ - ю...
com - be...
Я у - ми - ра - ю...
Viens à mon ai - de...
въ го - родъ.
vil - le.
Пой - демъ ско - рѣ - е!
Par - tons, Prin - ces - se!
V. I con sord.
rit.
pp

418 Moderato.
Нин.
Nin.
p
А...
Ah...
Чудаки
Les Ridicules
Какъ буд-то есть.
C'est bien pos-sible.
f
Тенорамъ.
Aux ténors.
Эй! по-слушайте, нѣтъ ли у васъ во - ды?
Eh! vous au-tres là, n'au - riez vous pas de l'eau?
418 Moderato.
T-be
f energico
pp
419
Чудаки (тенора) выносятъ
Les Ridicules (ténors) appor-
Пускай.
C'est bien.
Чуд.
Rid.
Ну, такъ дай-те ей. Пусть се-бѣ по - пьетъ.
Mais a-lors donnez donc, il faut qu'elle boive!
Fiati
mp
из башни ведро съ водою и ставятъ его посреди сцены. Затѣмъ возвращаются въ башню.
tent de la tour un seau d'eau et, l'ayant placé au milieu de la scène, retournent dans la tour.
cresc.
V. I
f
dim.

420 Poco meno mosso.

Нинетта
Ninette

pp

Сжаль - - ся...
Grâ - - ce...

Fag. dolente

pp

p poco rit.

V-le

Нин.
Nin.

Сжаль - - ся...
Grâ - - ce...

Picc.

pp

V. I c. sord.

pp dolce

Принцъ
Le Prince

p

Ка - ко - е го - - ре!..
Ah, c'est a - tro - - ce!..

Fag.

pp

421 Animato. Увидѣвъ ведро.
Remarquant le seau.

Пр.
Pr.

Вотъ_ во - да!
Tiens!_ de l'eau!

Cor. con sord.

V-ni

pp

mf

f

422

poco rit. *a tempo*

Пр. *Pr.*

Пей, — мо - я Прин - цес - - са! Пей —

Bois, — *ma douce Prin - ces - - se! Bois* —

f *colla parte*

ff Quart., Fiati, Triang. *mp*

rit. 423 **Andante.** Даетъ ей пить изъ ведра. *Il lui donne à boire dans le seau.*

Пр. *Pr.*

— сколь - ко хо - чешь.

— *cette eau fraî - che.*

pp *rit.* *pp* *cresc.* *mp*

Andantino.

424 **Нинетта,** выпивъ. ***Ninette,*** *ayant bu.*

p

Спа - си - бо, Принцъ. Ты спасъ ме - ня отъ смер - ти.

Mer - ci, mon Prince. Tu m'as sau - vé la vi - e

Cl. Cl. *pp* Cl. bas. *p* Arpa

425

Нин. *Nin.*

Ты вер - нулъ ме - ня изъ за - то - че - нья. —

et tu m'as sor - tie de l'es - cla - va - ge. —

Нин.
Nin.
rit.
Ты тотъ, ко-го я и-щу всю мо-ю жизнь.
C'est toi que j'ai at-ten-du de-puis tou-jours.
p
pp
rit.
Allegro.
426
Принцъ
Le Prince
p
Силъ не бы-ло, чтобъ у-дер-жать ме-ня въ мо-емъ стре-
Non, rien ne pou-vait m'ar-rê-ter dans mon é-lan vers
Cor.
pp
Пр.
Pr.
427
мле-ньи къ те-бѣ. Я не стра-шил-ся
toi, bien ai-mée! Je n'ai pas crains l'af-
fpp
Пр.
Pr.
гроз-ной Кре-он-ты, я пре-взо-шелъ кош-мар-ну-ю ку-
freu-se Cré-on-te, j'ai do-mi-né l'a-tro-ce cui-si-

428
Пр.
Pr.
хар - ку, я из - бѣгъ боль - шой мѣд - ной лож - - ки,
niè - re, j'ai bra - vé la lou - che mor - tel - - le,
V. I
p
T-be
Cor.
Cor.
T-be
429
я про - ник - нулъ въ жар - ку - ю кух - ню. Нѣтъ, нѣтъ, мо -
j'ai pas - sé l'en - fer qu'est sa cui - si - ne. Non! mon a -
cresc.
f
f
430
я лю - бовь силь - нѣ - е Кре - он - ты, жар - че кух - ни. Предъ
mour est fort, plus fort que Cré - onte, plus chaud que la cui - si - ne. De -
8
pp
p pizz., Ob. e Fag.
pochis. rit.
ней блѣд - нѣ - ла ку - хар - ка и о - пу - ска - лась лож - ка.
vant l'a - mour s'in - cli - nait la louche et trem - blait Cré - on - te.
Fl., Cl., pizz.
pp
pochis. rit.

Andantino.
431 Нинетта, просто.
Ninette, simplement.
pp
Ми - лыйПринцъ, я такъ те - бя жда - ла, я
O, monPrince, c'est toi que j'at - ten - dais, à
V. I con sord.
pp dolce
Celli
Нин.
Nin.
poco rit.
432
p
такъ те - бя люб - лю, я такъ съ то - бо - ю счаст - - -
toi est mon a - mour. Je suis telle - ment heu - reuse
pp
Лирики, мягкими движеніями появляются на сценѣ.
Les Lyriques, sans bruit apparaissent sur scène.
Драмъ, ли
Don_nez de
pp
432
Arpa glis.
pp
Fl.
poco rit.
pp
pp Quart., Arpa
Нин.
Nin.
- - - - ли - ва!
par toi!
Лир.
Lyr.
ри - че - скихъ драмъ! Ро_ман - ти - че - ской люб -
vrais drames ly - riques, ro_man_tiques, é - mo - tion -
gliss.
8
Celli espress.
3 5

433

Лир. / *Lyr.*

ви! Цвѣ - товъ, лу - - - ны!
nants! Des fleurs, la lune!

Чудаки, изъ башенъ, прикладывая пальцы къ губамъ.
Les Ridicules, des tours, en mettant les doigts sur les lèvres.

Ти-ше... у-хо-ди-те...
Si-len-ce... en si-len-ce...

Вы лю-би-те лю-бовь...
Si vous ai-mez l'a-mour...

433

Fl. Fag. Arpa glis. Cl., Ob. pizz.

Лир. / *Lyr.*

Нѣж-ныхъ по-цѣ-лу - - евъ!
Des mo-ments d'ex-ta - - se!

Чуд. / *Rid.*

Такъ не мѣшайте имъ лю-бить.
Ne troublez pas les a-mou-reux.

Ти-ше... у-мо-
Vi-te... re-par-

V. I V-le

Лирики мягко исчезаютъ.
Les Lyriques disparaissent sans bruit.
Чуд.
Rid.
ля-емъ васъ...
tez sans bruit...
V. I
pp
Fl.
V. I
p
Picc.
8
434 Allegro moderato.
Принцъ, торжественно.
Le Prince, solennellement.
И - демъ, Прин - цес - са, во дво - рецъ.
Par - tons, Prin - cesse, dans mon pa - lais.
pp poco rit.
f 6 Cor., Ob., Ob. c.-al. p
p
Нинетта
Ninette
435 Poco più mosso.
Что ты, Принцъ, въ та - кихъ о - де - ждахъ? Да ме -
Im - pos - sible en ce cos - tu - me. Que di -
V-ni, Fl.
pp
p
pp
Cell. e Fag. espress.
Нин.
Nin.
436
ня Ко - роль не пуститъ!
rait le Roi, ton pè - re?
Принцъ, рѣшительно.
Le Prince, d'un air décidé.
Не мо - жетъ не пу - стить!
Mon père n'a rien à dire!
436
Ob.
V. I
mf
p
mp
p dolce
p

Нин.
Nin.
Нѣтъ, Принцъ, пой - ди впе - редъ, пред - у - пре - ди от - ца
Non, Prin - ce, pars d'a - bord, vas pré - ve - nir le Roi.
Ob. c.-al. e Fag.
Fag. solo
Celli
437
poco rit.
pp
и при - не - си мнѣ цар - скі - я о - де - жды.
Tu m'ap - porte - ras aus - si une robe ro - ya - le.
Cl.
Ob.
Fl.
Camp.
colla parte
Fl., Cl., Arpa
poco rit.
a tempo
438
Я по - до - жду здѣсь.
Je t'at - ten - drai là.
Принцъ
Le Prince
Хо - ро - шо, я по - ви -
Si tu veux, je t'o - bé -
V. I
pizz.
Cl. bas.
Fag.
439 Pochissimo meno mosso (un poco maestoso).
Пр.
Pr.
ну - юсь.
is.
Но самъ Ко - роль прій - детъ на -
Le Roi vien - dra i - ci lui
6 Cor., Ob., Ob. c.-al.
f maestoso
mp

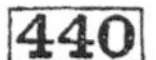

Нинетта, нѣжно.
Ninette, tendrement.

Про - щай, вер - нись ско - рѣ - е!
A - dieu, re - viens bien vi - te!

Пр.
Pr.

встрѣ - - - чу.
mê - - - me.

440

V-ni Pic.

fp *pp*

V-ni e V-le con sord.

Нин.
Nin.

Нѣжно.
Tendrement.

Уходитъ.
Il s'en va.

Про - щай, мо - я Прин - цес - са...
A - dieu, ma chère Prin - ces - se...

Andante assai.

441

Arpe, Fiati, V-ni.

p espress.

Celli, V-le

m.d. m.s.

Нинетта одна. Садится задумчиво на камень.
Ninette est seule. Pensive, elle s'assoit sur une pierre.

V-no solo sul G

pp

V. I

V-ni e Fl.

sempre pp

Cor.

442
Нинетта, мечтательно.
Ninette, rêveuse.
pp
О, как я счаст-ли-ва!..
O, que je suis heu-reuse!..
ten.
V.I
8
rit.
Arpa
dolcissimo
pp
m.d.
Andante.
443
На сценѣ почти ночь. Виденъ силуэтъ Смеральдины, которая крадется сзади къ Нинеттѣ. Позади Смеральдины появляет-ся силуэтъ Фаты Морганы.
Il fait presque nuit. On voit la silhouette de Sméraldine qui se glisse vers Ninette. Derrière Sméraldine apparaît la silhouette de Fata Morgana.
pp
Tam-tam pp
p
T-ni con sord. e G. Cassa
pesante
444
Чудаки, безпокойно.
Les Ridicules, inquiéts.
Сме-раль-ди-на...
Smé-ral-di-ne...
444
pp

Чуд.
Rid.
Съ бу_лав _ кой...
Une é _ pin _ gle...
mf 6 Corni
Фа _ та Мор_га _ _ _ _ _ _ _ _ на...
Fa _ ta Mor_ga _ _ _ _ _ _ _ _ na...
pp
Дѣ _ ло бу_ детъ
Ça de_vient bien
пло_ хо!
lou_che!
445
T-be e Cor.c.sord.
f
dim.
Cor. senza sord.
mp pesante

Волненіе Чудаковъ доходитъ до того, что они, выйдя изъ башенъ, на цыпочкахъ приближаются къ Нинеттѣ, дабы увидѣть, что произойдетъ.

L'inquiétude des Ridicules atteint un tel degré que, sortant des tours, ils s'approchent de Ninette, sur les pointes des pieds, pour voir ce qui se passera.

446

Allegro non troppo.

pp V-ni con sord.

pp

p

447

Ob.

mp

mp V. I e T-ba con sord.

mp

Смеральдина, подкравшись къ Нинеттѣ сзади, вонзаетъ ей въ голову большую волшебную булавку.
Sméraldine, s'étant glissée auprès de Ninette, lui enfonce dans la tête une grande épingle magique.

448 **Нинетта,** протяжно и жалобно восклицаетъ.
Ninette, gémissant longuement et plaintivement.

Нинетта исчезаетъ, превратившись въ крысу. Маленькая крыса черезъ всю сцену устремляется въ кулису.
449 *Ninette disparaît s'étant transformée en rat. Un petit rat à travers toute le scène se précipite dans la coulisse.*

Fag.

f

Quart. e T. mil.

Чудаки
Les Ridicules

f

Ай! Кры-са! Кры-са! Кры - са!
Aïe! diable! quel grand rat!

450

Чудаки, очень испугавшись крысы, спасаются въ башни.
Les Ridicules, très effrayés par le rat, se sauvent dans les tours.

f

Ай! Кры-са! Кры - са!
Aïe! diable! quel rat!

450

Cor. gliss.

f

T-ni

ff

8

3 3

8

T-ni

f

ff

451
Чудаки
f Les Ridicules
Фу, какъ про-
Pouah! c'est im-
f
451
f
3
3
Чуд.
Rid.
тив-но!
mon-de!
Кры-са!
Un rat!
452
452 veloce
f
mf V-le e Clar.
dim.
453
Чудаки
Les Ridicules
f
Бѣд-на-я Ни-
Mal-heu-reuse Ni-
f
453
p V-ni con sord.

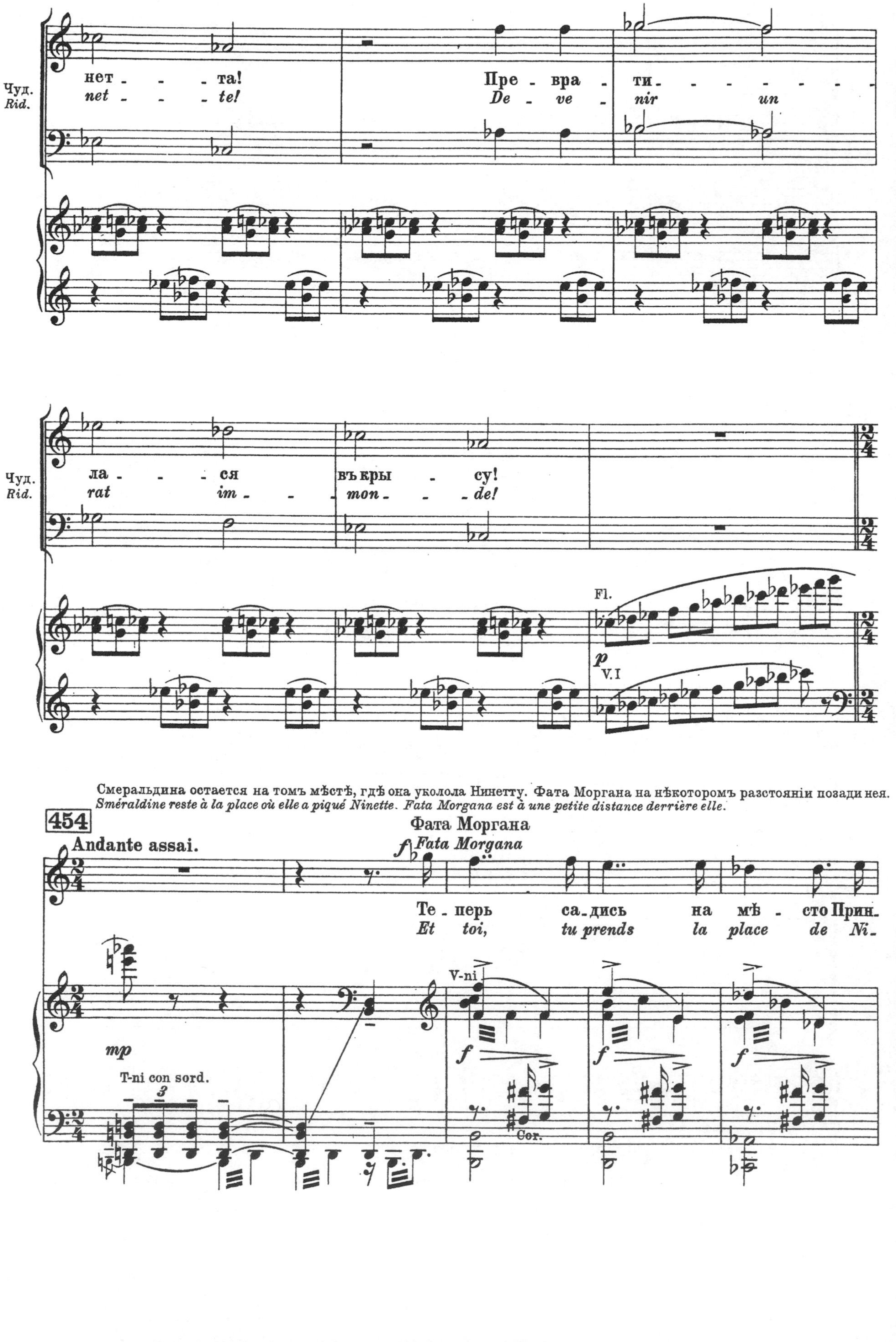

Чуд. *Rid.*

нет - - - та! Пре - вра - ти - - - - - - -
net - - - te! De - ve - nir un

Чуд. *Rid.*

ла - - - ся въ кры - су!
rat im - - - mon - - - de!

Fl. *p* V. I

Смеральдина остается на томъ мѣстѣ, гдѣ она уколола Нинетту. Фата Моргана на нѣкоторомъ разстоянiи позади нея.
Sméraldine reste à la place où elle a piqué Ninette. Fata Morgana est à une petite distance derrière elle.

455
Фата.
Fata.
mp
poco rit.
p
Исчезаетъ.
Elle disparaît.
цес - сы и го - во - ри, что ты Прин - цес - са.
net - te et dis - que tu es la vraie Prin - ces - se.
f
p Quart., Corni
poco rit.
T-be
pp
T-ni e Timp.
p
8va bassa
456 Tempo di Marcia animata.
3 T-be e 2 T-ni con sord., Piatti, Triang., T. mil., Arpe
pp
Tuba e C. F.
За кулисами звуки марша.
On entend une marche à la cantonade.
457
tacet
Появляется торжественное шествіе съ факелами и фонарями: Король, Принцъ, Клариче, Леандръ, Панталонъ, придворные, стража.
Un cortège pompeux apparaît avec des torches et des lanternes: le Roi, le Prince, Clarice, Léandre, Pantalon, des courtisans, les gardes.
Quart., Fl.
f
ff Tutti

458

3

3

Принцъ, радостно.
Le Prince, joyeusement.

459 Moderato.

Вотъ о-на! Вотъ мо-я Прин-цес-са!
Quel bon-heur! C'est ma belle Prin-ces-se!

Король
Le Roi

Та-ка-я Прин-цес-са?
Cette fem-me... Prin-ces-se?

459 Moderato.

f *f* *p* sul pontic., Piatti

Allegro moderato.

Смеральдина
Sméraldine

460

Принцъ
Le Prince

Э-то я, Прин-цес-са Ни-нет-та!
C'est bien moi. Je suis ta Ni-net-te.

Э-то не о-на!
Mais ce n'est pas elle!

460

Нѣтъ,
Non,

f *fp* Ob. *p* Fiati

pizz.

461

Смер.
Smér.

Пр.
Pr.

Принцъ, ты о-бѣ-
Prince, tu m'es li-

нѣтъ! Э-то злой об-манъ!
non! Quel af-freux men-songe!

V. I

461

f Quart. *f* V-le e Celli *mf* T-be e Cor. *p*

8

Arpa, Ob. c.-al.

Смер.
Smér.
щелъ на мнѣ же - нить - ся.
é par ta pro - mes - se.
Пр.
Pr.
На те - бѣ?
T'é - pou - ser?
Ни за
Non, ja -
f subito
462
что!
mais!
Король
Le Roi
Я не же - нюсь на ней!
Elle me dé - goûte, cette femme!
Я не - на -
Non, je re -
Сынъ мой...
Mon fils...
Сынъ мой...
Prin - ce...
V-ni, V-le
Timp.
ви - жу е - е!
fuse ce mariage!
463
Твердо.
Fermement.
Король
Roi
Принцъ! тво - е цар - ско - е
Prince! tu sais q'un Prince ro -
Cor., Ob., Ob. c.-al.

Король
Roi
464
сло - во не - пре - лож - - - - - - - но.
yal n'a qu'une pa - ro - - - - - - - le.
Celli, V-le
f feroce
Принцъ, ты о - бѣ - щалъ на ней же - нить - - - - ся,
Prince, tu es li - é par ton hon - neur.
465
Принцъ
Le Prince
На а - рап - кѣ?
Une né - gres - se?
Очень рѣшительно.
Très autoritaire.
и по - то - му
Tu l'é - pouse - ras,
же - нись!
j'ai dit!
Придворные, въ ужасѣ и удивленіи.
Les courtisans, surpris et épouvantés.
А!
Ah!
T-ni, Timp.

466
Растерянно.
Perplexe.
Пр.
Pr.
Грозно.
Terrible.
Ка - кой у - жасъ!
C'est ter - ri - ble!
Король
Roi
По - ве - лѣ - ва - - - - - - - - - ю!
Je te l'or - don - - - - - - - - - - ne!
466
T-ni, G.Cas.
467
По - ве - лѣ - ва - - - - - - - - - - - - ю!
Je te l'or - don - - - - - - - - - - - - ne!
T-ba
По - дай ей ру - ку.
Donne lui le bras.
G.P.
Ше - ствi - е, впе -
Le cortè - ge en
Шествiе отправляется обратно. Принца, который въ отчаянiи, заставляютъ подать руку Смеральдинѣ.
Le cortège rebrousse chemin. On force le Prince, qui est au désespoir, à donner le bras à Sméraldine.
468
Tempo di Marcia animata.
редъ!
marche!
T-ba con sord.
p marcatissimo
T-ba con sord.

Подаетъ руку Клариче и слѣдуетъ за шествіемъ.
Il tend le bras à Clarice et suit le cortège.

Леан.
Léan.

цес-са вышла чер-на-я.
cesse en est sortie toute noire.

Занавѣсъ.
Rideau.

Fag.

p T-ni

f

ff Tutti

АКТЪ IV.

КАРТИНА I.

При поднятiи занавѣса, вмѣсто декорацiи, виденъ второй занавѣсъ, кабалистическiй, какъ во II картинѣ перваго акта.

ACTE IV.

TABLEAU I.

Après le lever du rideau, au lieu du décor, on voit un second rideau, cabalistique, comme au second tableau du premier acte.

473
Челій
Tchélio
Ахъ!
Ah!
Не - год - на - я вѣдь - ма, не -
I - gno - ble sor - ciè - re, i -
Cor. Quart.
Fiati e col legno
Чел.
Tchél.
год - на - я вѣдь - ма, низ - ка - я кол - ду - нья, низ - ка - я кол - ду - нья, у -
gno - ble sor - ciè - re, lâche et mi - sé - ra - ble, lâche et mi - sé - ra - ble! Tu
бо - го - е ис - ча - ді - е а - да, ис -
as é - té ra - tée par le dia - ble, ra -
T-be con sord.
V. I con sord.
474
Фата Моргана
Fata Morgana
Ахъ, ты, магъ на - пы - жен - ный, магъ на - пы - жен - ный,
Oh, toi, vieux sor - cier pré - ten - tieux, sor - cier pré - ten -
ча - ді - е а - да, ис - ча - ді - е а - да, ис - ча - ді - е а - - -
tée par le dia - ble, ra - tée par le dia - ble, ra - tée par le dia - - -

Фата.
Fata.
магъ на_ду_тый, магъ на_ду_тый, магъ, ко_то_ро_му ни_
tieux, sans for_ce, sans puis_san_ce, ma_gi_cien que per_
Чел.
Tchél.
_ да! Стыд_но, стыд_но,
_ ble! Lâ_che, lâ_che,
Cl.
475
кто не по_ви_ну_ет_ся!
sonne n'é_coute ja_mais, ja_mais!
стыд
lâche
V.I
_но те_бѣ, пад_ша_я вѣдь_ма, пад_ша_я вѣдь_ма, из_мель_чать до
cré_a_ture! Tu n'as pas hon_te de t'a_bais_ser à te ser_vir d'é_
V-ni, Fl.
p col legno, Fiati

476
Фата Моргана
Fata Morgana
А ты... а ты... а ты, без.слав.ный
Et toi... et toi... et toi, sor.cier sans
Чел.
Tchél.
жен.скихъ бу.ла.вокъ, гад.кихъ бу.ла.вокъ, от.рав.лен.ныхъ бу.ла.вокъ!
pin.gles de fem.mes, vi.les é.pin.gles, é.pingles em.poi.son.né.es!
V. I
Fl.
476
fp
f
Фата.
Fata.
магъ, какъ ты смѣ.шонъ, смѣ.шонъ, смѣ.шонъ съ тво.и.ми бан.ти.ка.ми! Ха.ха.ха.ха!
gloire, tu es gro.tesque a.vec tes p'tits ru.bans de soie ma.gi.ques! Ha.ha.ha.ha!
477
Стыд.но!
Lâ.che!
mp
p
Picc.
mf
T-ba
Бан.ти.ка.ми! Ха.ха.ха.ха.ха! Кол.ду.етъ бан.томъ! Ты
C'est gro.tes.que! Ha.ha.ha.ha.ha! Quel im.bé.ci.le! Tu
Низ.ко! Ко.летъ бу.лав.кой! Мерз.ко!
Lâ.che! Lâ.che! Quelle hon.te! Dia.ble!
ff
f Xylo.

478

Фата. *Fata.*

магъ для раз-вле-че-нi-я мо-ло-день-кихъ дѣ-вицъ!
n'es qu'un ma-gi-cien pour a-mu-ser des jeu-nes filles!

Отъ взмаха руки Челiя молнiя и ударъ грома.
D'un mouvement de main Tchélio provoque un éclair et un coup de tonnerre.

dim.

Tam-tam

Челiй
Tchélio

Ста-ра-я фу-рi-я, ты не рѣ-ши-лась да-же
Vieil-le fu-ri-e, par cou-ar-dise tu n'as même

Fiati

V-ni

V-le

479

Фата Моргана
Fata Morgana

Без-чест-ный ча-ро-дѣй!
Tu n'es qu'un mal-hon-nête,

Чел. *Tchél.*

дѣй-ство-вать са-ма!
pas a-gi toi meme!

Отъ взмаха руки Фаты Морганы молнiя и громъ.
D'un mouvement de main Fata Morgana provoque un éclair et un coup de tonnerre.

Ты под-сы-
Tu t'es ser-

479

T-be con sord.

T-ni con sord.

Tam-tam

Фата.
Fata.
Иль ты за-былъ, что судь - бу тво-ихъ лю-бимцевъ про-иг-ралъ мнѣ
car tu ou-blies que tu as per-du aux car-tes le des-tin du
Чел.
Tchél.
ла - ешь чер-ну-ю а - рап - ку,
vie d'une sale es-cla-ve noi - re,
Отъ взмаха руки Челія молнія и громъ.
Eclair et tonnerre provoqués par Tchélio.
p
fp
480
Фата Моргана тѣснитъ Челія.
Fata Morgana fait reculer Tchélio.
въ кар - ты? О - ни мо - и! О - ни мо -
Prin - - ce. Il est à moi! Il est à
гряз-ну-ю а - рап - ку!
d'une es-cla-ve noi - re!
Фата взмахиваетъ. Молнія и громъ.
Eclair et tonnerre provoqués par Fata.
T-ba
T-ni
f
Cor.
T-ne
Еще разъ.
Encore.
481
ff
и! Спа-са - я ихъ, ты лѣ-зешь мнѣ въ кар-
moi! En les sau vant tu voles comme un tri -
Arpa gliss.
espress.

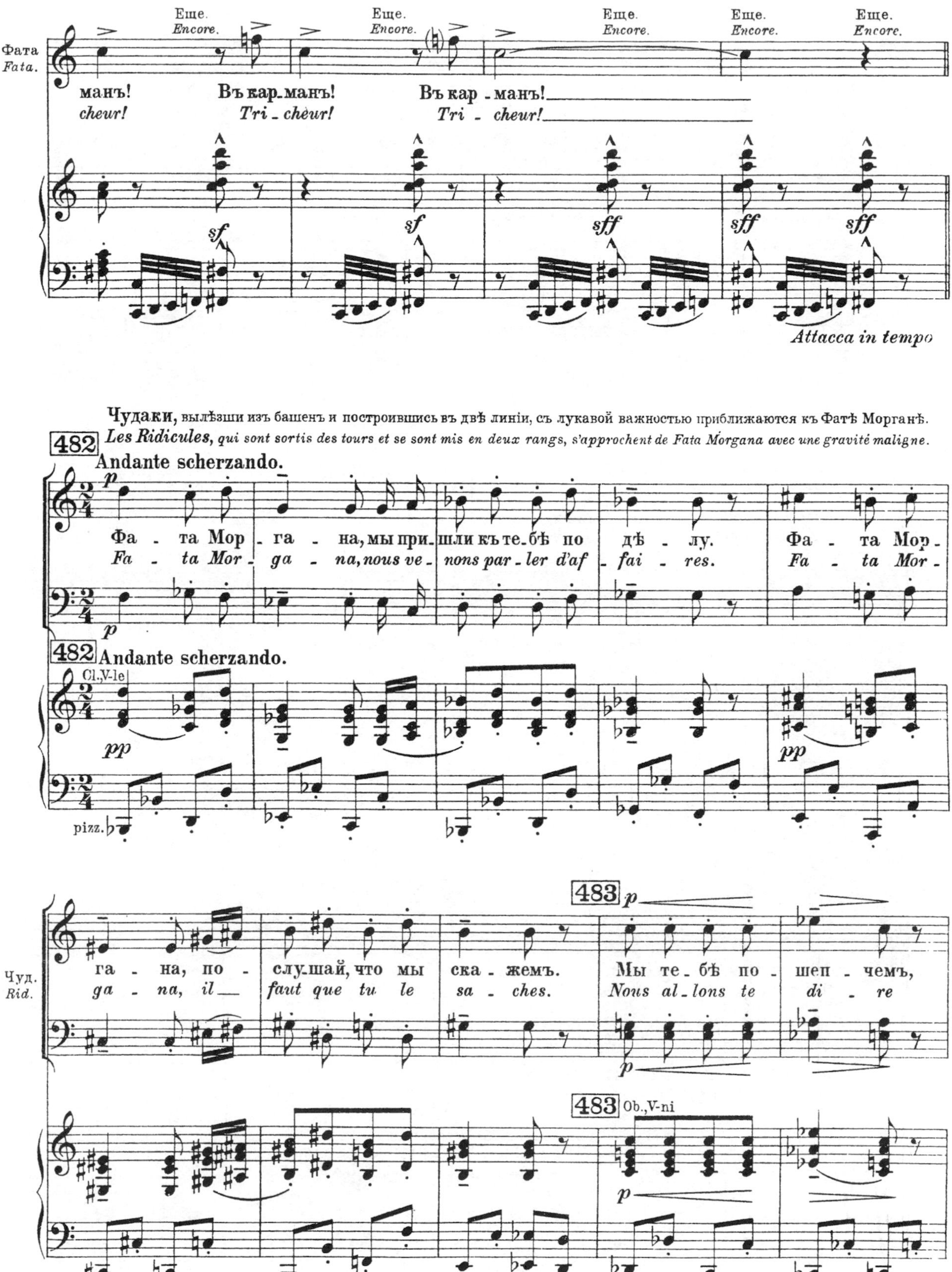

Чудаки, вылѣзши изъ башенъ и построившись въ двѣ линіи, съ лукавой важностью приближаются къ Фатѣ Морганѣ.
Les Ridicules, *qui sont sortis des tours et se sont mis en deux rangs, s'approchent de Fata Morgana avec une gravité maligne.*

482 **Andante scherzando.**

p

Фа - та Мор - га - на, мы при - шли къ те - бѣ по дѣ - лу. Фа - та Мор -
Fa - ta Mor - ga - na, nous ve - nons par - ler d'af - fai - res. Fa - ta Mor -

482 **Andante scherzando.**

Cl., V-le

pp

pizz.

Чуд.
Rid.

га - на, по - слу_шай, что мы ска - жемъ. Мы те - бѣ по - шеп - чемъ,
ga - na, il faut que tu le sa - ches. Nous al - lons te di - re

483 p

483 Ob., V-ni

p

Чуд.
Rid.
мы чуть-чуть по - шеп - чемъ, такъ, не-множ-ко, нѣ-сколь-ко сло - ве - чекъ.
une nou-velle cu - rieu - se, nous la chu-chote-rons à ton o - reil - le.
По -
Ap -
Ob., V-ni
484
По - ди же по - бли - же, по - ди же по - бли - же, по - слу - шай,
Ap - pro - che, en - co - re, ap - pro - che, en - co - re, é - cou - te,
ди же по - бли - же, по - ди же по - бли - же, по - слу - шай, что
pro - che, en - co - re, ap - pro - che, en - co - re, é - cou - te, c'est
Cl.
485
что ска - жемъ, по - слу - шай, что ска - жемъ. Фа - та Мор - га - на!
c'est gra - ve, é - cou - te, c'est gra - ve. Fa - ta Mor - ga - na!
ска - жемъ, по - слу - шай, что ска - жемъ.
gra - ve, é - cou - te, c'est gra - ve.
V-le pizz.
Cl.
V-ni pizz., Arpe, Fl.

486 Allegro moderato.
Чуд.
Rid.
Фа - та Мор - га - на!
Fa - ta Mor - ga - na!
Гопъ!!
Hop!!
Неожиданно вталкиваютъ ее въ одну изъ башенъ и запираютъ. Изъ башни огонь и дымъ.
Brusquement ils la poussent dans une des tours et l'enferment. De la tour sort du feu et de la fumée.
486 Allegro moderato.
V-ni, Fl., Picc.
T-be, Cor., T-ni, Triang., T. mil.
Piatti
487
Чудаки, Челію.
Les Ridicules, à Tchélio.
Ну, те - перь ско -
Va, mainte - nant tu
487 Quart., Fl.
m.d.
G. Cassa
Чуд.
Rid.
рѣй спа - сай тво - ихъ лю - бим - цевъ!
peux sau - ver ta cour ro - ya - le!

488 L'istesso tempo. (♩= ♩.)

T-be e T-ni con sord.

Челій, дѣлая страшные заклинательные жесты по направленію къ башнѣ, гдѣ заперта Фата Моргана.

Tchélio, fait de terribles gestes d'incantation vers la tour où est enfermée Fata Morgana.

489

Пом - ни, вѣдь - - - ма, какъ гро - зенъ Магъ Че - -

Vois, sor - ciè - - - re, quelle est ma puis - san - -

Cor., Fag., Ob. c-al.

C. F. e Tuba

490 Проваливается съ огнемъ и дымомъ.

Il s'engouffre avec feu et fumée.

Чел.
Tchél.

лій!
ce!

V-ni

Cor.

T-ne, Tuba e G. Cas.

491 **Чудаки,** возвращаясь въ башни, добродушно.

***Les Ridicules,** rentrant dans les tours, avec une bonhomie légèrement ironique.*

То - то...
Tiens, tiens...

гро - зенъ!..
puis - san - ce!..

Кабалистическій занавѣсъ поднимается.

Le rideau cabalistique se lève.

491

Cor.

Celli, Bassi

Attacca

КАРТИНА II.

Ярко освѣщенная тронная зала королевскаго дворца. Налѣво, на большомъ возвышеніи, тронъ Короля. Рядомъ два трона для Принца и будущей Принцессы. Надъ тремя тронами большой бархатный шатеръ, который можетъ быть задернутъ. Церемоніймейстеръ, слуги. Залъ постепенно наполняется придворными.

TABLEAU II.

La salle du trône du palais royal brillamment éclairée. A gauche, sur une grande estrade, le trône du Roi, auprès duquel deux trônes, l'un pour le Prince, l'autre pour la future Princesse. Au dessus des trois trônes un grand baldaquin en velours qui peut se fermer. Le Maître de Cérémonies, des serviteurs. La salle se remplit de courtisans.

Маршъ за кулисами.
Une marche à la cantonade
2 T-be e 3 T-ni con sord.,
Piat., Trian., T. mil., Arpa
p
494
p
dim.
pp
pizz.
mp
cresc.
f
tacet
mp
V-ni, Fl.
mp
f
T. mil.

Входитъ шествіе. Впереди Король. За нимъ Принцъ и Смеральдина. Далѣе Панталонъ, Клариче, придворные, стража.
Le cortège entre. Le Roi en tête, après lui le Prince et Sméraldine, puis Pantalon, Clarice, les courtisans et les gardes.

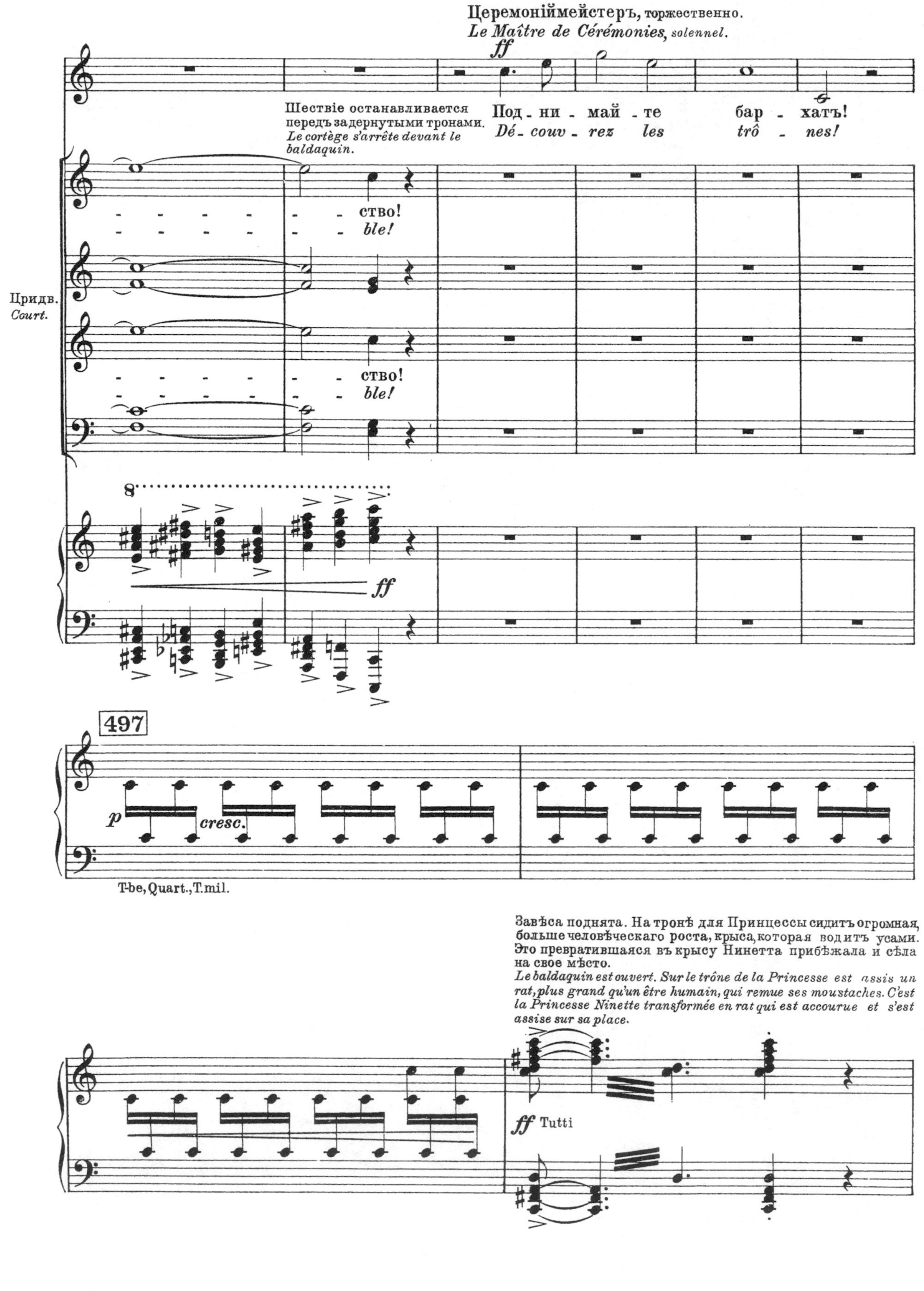

Церемоніймейстеръ, торжественно.
Le Maître de Cérémonies, solennel.

ff

Шествіе останавливается передъ задернутыми тронами.
Le cortège s'arrête devant le baldaquin.

Под - ни - май - те бар - хатъ!
Dé - couv - rez les trô - nes!

- - - - - - ство!
- - - - - - *ble!*

Придв.
Court.

- - - - - - ство!
- - - - - - *ble!*

8

ff

497

p *cresc.*

T-be, Quart., T.mil.

Завѣса поднята. На тронѣ для Принцессы сидитъ огромная, больше человѣческаго роста, крыса, которая водитъ усами. Это превратившаяся въ крысу Нинетта прибѣжала и сѣла на свое мѣсто.
Le baldaquin est ouvert. Sur le trône de la Princesse est assis un rat, plus grand qu'un être humain, qui remue ses moustaches. C'est la Princesse Ninette transformée en rat qui est accourue et s'est assise sur sa place.

Всѣ въ страшной растерянности отступаютъ на шагъ. Нѣкоторые придворные хватаются за оружіе, но всѣ испуганы.
Tous en grand désarroi reculent d'un pas. Plusieurs courtisans saisissent leurs armes.

499
Смер.
Smér.
страш-но!
ri - ble!
Церем.
M. de C.
страш-но!
ri - ble!
Пант.
Pant.
Ско-рѣ-е стра - жу!
Ap-pelez les gar - des!
Появляется освѣщенный Магъ Челій и заклинаетъ крысу съ отчаянными жестами.
Le Magicien Tchélio apparaît, éclairé. Il essaie de désenchanter le rat par des gestes desespérés.
Челій, заклинаетъ.
Tchélio, incantant.
Кры - са, Кры - са, пре-вра-тись об-рат - но въ Прин-
Rat, j'e - xi - ge que tu re-de-vien-nes Prin-
Придв.
Cour.
страш-но!
ri - ble!
499
f Quart.
p f

Король
Le Roi
Стра - - жа!
Gar - - des!
Стрѣ-ляй - - те!
Aux ar - - mes!
Чел.
Tchél.
цес - су!
ces - se!
Пре-вра-тись въ Прин-цес-су!
Re-de-viens Prin-ces-se!
За - кли-
Je l'or-
pizz., col legno e T. mil.
500
Кор.
Roi.
Стрѣ-ляй-те!
Aux ar-mes!
Чел.
Tchél.
на - ю!
don - ne!
За - кли-на - ю!
Je l'or-don - ne!
Шумно вбѣгаетъ стража.
Les gardes accourent bruyamment.
un poco accelerando
Fag.
Ob.c.al.
cresc.
gliss.
Стража стрѣ-ляетъ.
Les gardes tirent.
Timp. soli.
Крыса превращается въ Принцессу Нинетту. Магъ Челій исчезаетъ.
Le rat redevient la Princesse Ninette. Le Magicien Tchélio disparaît.
a tempo
dim.

Poco più largamente.(Moderato).
Принцъ, бросается къ Нинеттѣ.
Le Prince, se précipitant vers Ninette.
501
ff
О - на, о-
C'est elle, c'est
Церемонiймейстеръ
Le Maître de Cérémonies
f
Что за чу-до!
Quel mi-ra-cle!
Панталонъ
Pantalon
f
Что за чу-до!
Quel mi-ra-cle!
Король
Le Roi
f
Что за чу-до!
Quel mi-ra-cle!
f
f
Придворные
Les courtisans
Что за чу-до!
Quel mi-ra-cle!
f
f
Чудаки, съ радостнымъ удивленiемъ.
Les Ridicules, avec un étonnement joyeux.
p
Прин-цес-са Ни-нет-та?!
Prin-ces-se Ni-net-te?
p
Poco più largamente.(Moderato).
501
V.I
pp pizz.
ff
passionato
f

На колѣняхъ предъ Нинеттой
и хватая ея руки.
A genoux devant Ninette en lui
tenant les mains.
Пр.
Pr.
на, мо - я Прин - цес - са! Мо - я лю -
elle, c'est ma Prin - ces - se! C'est mon a -
m.d.
m.s.
p
Cl.e Arpa
бовь! Мой а - пель - синъ!
mour! C'est mon o - range!
502
Придворные
Les courtisans
Ка -
Grands
Celli
mp espress.
mf espress.
cresc.
f
Bassi

Король
Le Roi
503
Я у-див-ленъ.
Je suis sur-pris.
Придв.
Cour.
ка-я кра-си-ва-я Прин-цес-са!
dieux! qu'elle est bel-le, la Prin-ces-se!
503
f
p
pp
T-ni
pizz., Fag., Ob. c.-al.
Принцъ, разнѣженно.
Le Prince, avec mollesse.
504
pp
Ни-нет-та...
Ni-net-te...
Кор.
Roi.
Но Прин-цес-са не-дур-на.
Mais elle n'est vrai-ment pas mal.
V.I, Fl., Cl., Cor.
Cl.bas.
504
p
mp
Cl. e Cl.bas.
pp
Bassi

505 Allegro.
Труффальдино, появляясь неизвѣстно откуда.
Trouffaldino, arrivant on ne sait d'où.
Указывая на Смеральдину.
En désignant Sméraldine.
Король.
Roi.
А кто же э - то?
A - lors cette fem - me?
Э - то Сме - раль -
Mais c'est Smé - ral -
Allegro.
505
Fl., Ob., Cl.
pizz.
Cl.
dim.
Клариче
Clarice
506
Смераль - ди - на?!
Sméral - di - ne?!
Труф.
Trouf.
ди - на!
di - ne!
Леандръ
Léandre
Смераль - ди - на?!
Smé - ral - di - ne?!
Сме - раль - ди - на?
Smé - ral - di - ne?
Тай - на -
N'est elle
Fag. e C. Fag.
Fag. e Celli sul pontic.
Леан.
Léan.
Дѣлая шагъ впередъ.
En faisant un pas en avant.
507
Ко - роль...
Mon Roi...
Не слыша Леандра.
N'entendant pas Léandre.
я со - общ - ни - ца Ле - ан - дра?
pas com - pli - ce de Lé - an - dre?
Я на - чи -
Oui, je com -
cresc.
Cor. con sord.

508 Andante non tropo.
Леан.
Léan.
Ко-роль...
Mon Roi...
Гнѣвно и презрительно.
En colère et avec dédain.
Король.
Roi.
на-ю по-ни-мать.
mence à tout com-prendre.
Мол-чи!
Tais toi!
Ты пре-да-тель!
Tu es un traî-tre!
Andante non troppo.
508
mp
pizz.
fp
Ob., Arpa, V-ni pizz.
Кларичe, взволнованно.
Clarice, émotionnée.
Дя-дя...
On-cle...
О-той-ди!
Va-t'en!
Тво-и
Je sais,
ру-ки ис-пач-ка-ны я-домъ.
tu as trempé dans le cri-me.
Придворные
Les courtisans
Преда-тель...
Un traî-tre...
mf
p

509
Я - - домъ...
Cri - - me...
Король, въ торжественномъ гнѣвѣ, поднимается къ трону. Всѣ въ трепетѣ.
Le Roi, dans une colère solennelle, monte vers le trône. Tous restent figés de peur.
Придв.
Court.
Я - домъ...
Cri - me...
509
Cor.
Страшна - я ми - ну - та...
Quel mo - ment d'an - gois - se...
Онъ рѣ - ша - етъ...
Il dé - ci - de...
Придв.
Court.
cresc.

Король, величественно.
Roi, majestueusement.
510
ff
По - - ве - лѣ - ва - - - ю:
Je don - ne l'or - - - dre:
8
ff
m.s.
pesante
Ped.
Ped.
511
Смеральдина въ ужасѣ, отступаетъ на шагъ.
Sméraldine, terrifiée, recule d'un pas.
Король.
Roi.
а - рап - ку Сме - раль - ди - - - ну,
l'es - cla - ve Smé - ral - di - - - ne,
8
Ob. c.-al., Fag.
Bassi
fp
Celli
Леандръ отступаетъ на шагъ.
Léandre recule d'un pas.
Король.
Roi.
ми - нист - ра Ле - ан - - - дра
le traî - - tre Lé - an - - - dre
Bassi
fp
Celli

512
Король
Roi.
и мо - ю пле - мян - ни - цу Кла - ри - - -
et sa lâche com - pli - ce, ma nièce Cla - ri - - -
accelerando
Ob., Ob. c.-al.
cresc.
fp
T-be con sord.

513
Клариче отступаетъ на шагъ.
Clarice recule d'un pas.
Король.
Roi.
- - - че
- - - ce,
по - вѣ - сить.
qu'on les pen - de.
a tempo
ff
f
G. P.
Панталонъ, Труффальдино, Церемоніймейстеръ, придворные, стража- всѣ падаютъ на колѣни.
Pantalon, Trouffaldino, le Maître de Cérémonies, les courtisans et les gardes tombent à genoux.
514 Moderato.
Трагическимъ шопотомъ.
Murmurant tragiquement.
По - вѣ - сить...
Qu'on les pen - de...
p T-be e Cor. con sord., Quart. sul pontic.
pp
Bassi, Timp.
Труффальдино, на колѣняхъ; сладко.
Trouffaldino, à genoux; d'une voix mielleuse.
515
Ко - роль, про - сти ихъ!
O Roi, par - donne les!
Панталонъ, толкаетъ его.
Pantalon, le poussant.
Мол - чи!
Tais toi!
p Quart.
p

Король, трагическимъ шопотомъ, утвердительно.
Le Roi, murmure affirmativement.
По - вѣсить...
Qu'on les pen_de...
Энергично.
Energiquement aux gardes.
Стра - жа, ве - рев_ку!
Gar - des, la cor_de!
Чудаки, подъ сильнымъ впечатлѣніемъ.
Les Ridicules, très impressionnés.
pp
По - вѣсить...
Les pendres...
pp
pp T-ba e T-ni
pp
G. P.
f Cor.
ff
Allegro.
516
Стража направляется къ нимъ. Смеральдина бросается бѣжать. Клариче за нею. Леандръ за Клариче. Стража устремляется въ погоню. Панталонъ, Труффальдино, Церемоніймейстеръ и всѣ придворные за стражей. Остаются: Король на ступеняхъ трона, Нинетта на своемъ тронѣ и Принцъ, все обнимающій ея колѣни.
Les gardes se dirigent vers eux. Sméraldine essaye de fuir, Clarice la suit, Léandre suit Clarice. Les gardes se jettent à leur poursuite. Pantalon, Trouffaldino, le Maître de Cérémonies et tous les courtisans se précipitent après les gardes. Il ne reste que le Roi sur les marches du trône, Ninette sur son trône et le Prince toujours embrassant ses genoux.
Quart.
f con fuoco

517
Труффальдино
Trouffaldino
Дер-жи ихъ!
A droi-te!
Церемон.
M. d. Cérémonies
Дер-жи ихъ!
A droi-te!
Панталонъ
Pantalon
Дер-жи ихъ!
A droi-te!
Дер - жи!
Te - nez!
Дер-жи!
A gauche!
Придв.
Court.
517
Fiati
Cor.
Cor., T-ne

Всѣ длинной цѣпью бѣгутъ на авансцену и въ лѣвую кулису. Затѣмъ появляются вглубинѣ сцены изъ лѣвой кулисы и въ томъ же порядкѣ бѣгутъ черезъ всю сцену въ правую кулису.

Tous en longues chaînes courent vers l'avant-scène et dans la coulisse de gauche, puis apparaissent au fond de la scène de la coulisse gauche et dans le même ordre courent à travers toute la scène dans la coulisse droite.

519

Cl., Ob. c.-al.

V-ni, Pic., Fl., Ob.

fp

cresc.

ff Quart. e Fiati

520

f Quart. spic.

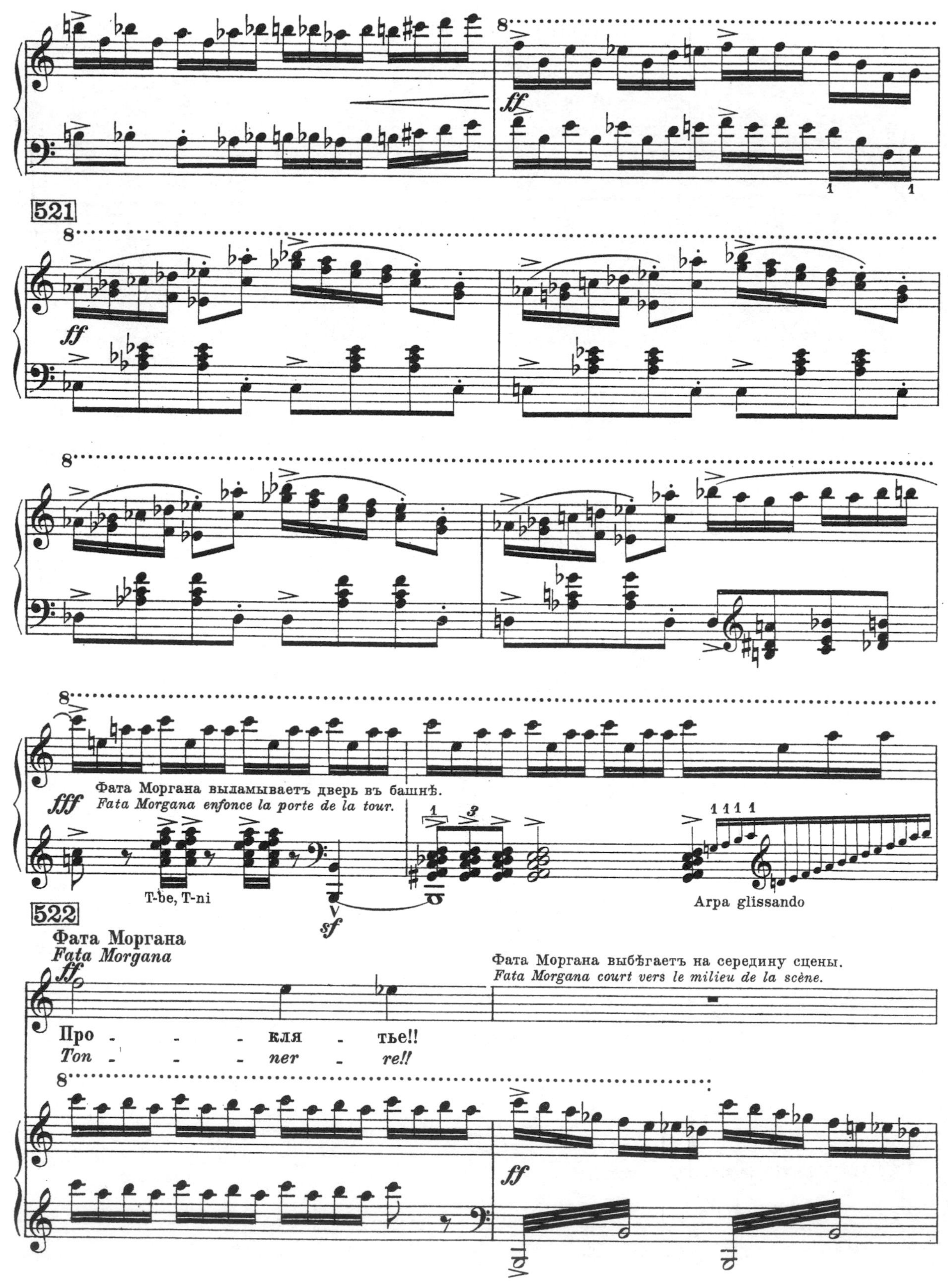
521
Фата Моргана выламываетъ дверь въ башнѣ.
Fata Morgana enfonce la porte de la tour.
T-be, T-ni
Arpa glissando
522
Фата Моргана
Fata Morgana
Фата Моргана выбѣгаетъ на середину сцены.
Fata Morgana court vers le milieu de la scène.
Про - - - кля - тье!!
Ton - - - ner - re!!

Фата.
Fata.
Ско-рѣй! Ко мнѣ! Въ мо-и объ-я-тья!
Ve-nez à moi, je vous pro-tè-ge!
Бѣгущіе вновь появляются на сценѣ изъ правой кулисы и устремляются къ Фатѣ Морганѣ. Передъ нею открывается люкъ.
Les poursuivis et les poursuivants réapparaissent sur scène de la coulisse droite et courent vers Fata Morgana. Devant elle s'ouvre une trappe.
523
Quart.
Fiati
T-ni e pizz.
Quart.

Andante assai.
Смеральдина, за нею Клариче и Леандръ прыгаютъ въ люкъ, откуда огонь и дымъ. Фата Моргана проваливаетсявслѣдъ за ними.
Sméraldine, puis Clarice et Léandre sautent dans la trappe d'où sort du feu et de la fumée. Fata Morgana s'y engouffre après eux.
524
V-ni, Fiati, Camp., Xyl.
ff T-ni, Cor., Tam-tam
Cor., T-ni
ff
Cor.
p
Прибѣжавшіе стража и придворные окружаютъ пустое и ровное мѣсто.
Les gardes et les courtisans accourus, encerclent la place maintenant vide.
525
Ob. e V. I con sord.
p
Cor.
Bassi, Cor., Cl. bas.
Труффальдино
Trouffaldino
p
Гдѣ же из - мѣн - ни - ки?
Traî - tres, où êtes vous donc?
Церемон.
M. d. Cérémonies
p
Гдѣ же из - мѣн - ни - ки?
Traî - tres, où êtes vous donc?
Панталонъ
Pantalon
p
Гдѣ же из - мѣн - ни - ки?
Traî - tres, où êtes vous donc?
pp
pp
Придворные
Les courtisans
Гдѣ же из - мѣн - ни - ки?
Traî - tres, où êtes vous donc?
pp
pp
T-be
pp
Cl.

526
Andante maestoso (Poco più mosso).
Труффальдино
Trouffaldino
ff
Да
Bé -
Церемон.
M. d Cérémonies
ff
Да
Bé -
Панталонъ
Pantalon
ff
Да
Bé -
Король
Le Roi
Да здравствуетъ Принцъ и Принцес-са!
Non, vive le Prince et la Prin-ces-se!
Придв.
Court.
Чудаки, превозглашаютъ.
Les Ridicules, entonnent.
Да здравствуетъ Ко-роль!
Cri - ez donc: vive le Roi!
526
Andante maestoso (Poco più mosso).
Cor.
sff
Cor.

527
Труф.
Trouf.
здравству-етъ Ко - роль, Принцъ и Прин - цес - - - са!
nis soit no-tre Roi, le Prince et la Prin - ces - - - se!
Церем.
M. d. C.
Пант.
Pant.
Придв.
Court.
Чуд.
Rid.
527
Tutti
Занавѣсъ.
Rideau.
Конецъ.
La Fin.